The Story of Alpha:
A Multiage, Student-Centered Team—
33 Years and Counting

by Susan Kuntz

NMSA

National Middle School Association
Westerville, Ohio

National Middle School Association
4151 Executive Parkway, Suite 300
Westerville, Ohio 43081
1-800-528-NMSA
www.nmsa.org

Sue Swaim, Executive Director
Jeff Ward, Deputy Executive Director
April Tibbles, Director of Publications
Edward Brazee, Editor, Professional Publications
John Lounsbury, Consulting Editor
Mary Mitchell, Designer, Editorial Assistant
Mark Shumaker, Cover Design
Dawn Williams, Production Specialist
Marcia Meade-Hurst, Senior Publications Representative

Library of Congress Cataloging-in-Publication Data
Kuntz, Susan, date.
   The story of Alpha: a multiage, student-centered team, 33 years and counting/by Susan Kuntz.
         p. cm
   Includes bibliographical references.
   ISBN: 1-56090-177-2 (pbk.)
   1. Middle school education--Vermont. 2. Educational innovations--Vermont. 3. Shelburne Community School (Shelburne, Vt.) I. Title.
LB1623.52.V47K86 2005
373.743'17--dc22   2004060965

Contents

Acknowledgements

Without the vision of many educators in Shelburne, Vermont, the Alpha Program would not have developed as it did. Particularly I want to thank John Winton, Jim Reid, Susan Wanner, and the special teacher who carried the vision for 25 years, Carol Smith. The courage, creativity, and energy of these educators made Alpha worth writing about.

I am deeply indebted to the students from Alpha. Their "school stories" made me understand what matters to them. They cared enough about the larger purpose of this endeavor to trust me with their ideas and words. Alpha is their story.

John Lounsbury and Mary Mitchell at NMSA deserve special thanks for their guidance and detailed attention to the preparation of this manuscript for publication.

Finally, I am grateful to my family, Norb, Jack, Katie, and Aaron, whose lives I am fortunate to share and whose Alpha stories I have lived. It is to them that I dedicate this book.

— Susan Kuntz
October 2004

FOREWORD

A Vision of
Middle Level Education Manifest

Recently I met three other new retirees at a social gathering. Inevitably conversation turned to exchanges about our respective careers. On learning that I had been a middle level teacher, principal and teacher educator, the other three unhesitatingly launched into impassioned pronouncements about "what schools oughta be doing." One insisted on "a solid foundation in physics for every child and strictly enforced discipline in every school." Another countered that "mathematics defines how things work" and "students need to understand algebra and calculus" (which he later offered were his best subjects in college). The third preached about the importance of learning how to get others to do their work—whatever the work might be—to high standards (he lamented the poor preparation of entry level employees in the business he owned).

I was somewhat taken aback by how quickly an incidental disclosure of my professional career had precipitated such strongly held opinions from new acquaintances. Their confidence in their dogma was explicit. Two of them had careers in the sciences, yet there were no questions soliciting best evidence about successful schooling. In fact, the exchange never really became a conversation— just a brief but intense bombardment of contrasting opinions that benefitted no one. Reflecting on the incident later, I was annoyed with myself for several clever comments I might have made if I'd just been able to think more quickly.

Thankfully, Susan Kuntz has given us in this volume a perfect response for people who reflexively decree absolute truths about public education, truths drawn exclusively from personal empiricism. In her informative and refreshing history of Alpha—a truly remarkable and enduring middle level program—Kuntz teaches how a concept of education for young adolescents can weather the inevitable squalls of bias that so often sweep through public schools. She carefully explains how Alpha's teachers have turned popular criticisms such as "basic competencies" of two decades ago and the "standards movement" of today into positive initiatives grounded in teachers' understanding and commitment to accommodate their students' readiness and capacity for learning. The Alpha teachers' clear educational vision and commitment to child-centered schooling, restraint in the face of ideological attacks, and savvy about how to survive politically without compromising principles stands as a preeminent lesson in professional conduct to all teachers at every level. Most remarkable, perhaps, is that these qualities have been manifest through several generations of Alpha teachers. One teacher, Jim Reid, conceptualized and originated Alpha; Carol Smith sustained it for 25 years; and their dozen or so fellow teachers have never wavered from the original beliefs about educating young adolescents.

Although this publication was not intended as a handbook about how to organize and teach as a partner team, it includes an enormous amount of content detailing Alpha routines and traditions. Themes about ways students learn are unmistakable and include a remarkable array of resources, academic skills, citizenship essential to living in a democratic school community, and personal values of initiative, responsibility, and accountability. Heartwarming traditions are explained—the daily team meetings, the "Pig-out," sleepover, annual quilt project, spring trip, and especially the irresistible Candlelight Ceremony that commemorates students' third and final year on the team. I have rarely observed education that so clearly and meaningfully accommodates young adolescents' appreciation for recognition and affirmation that is so natural in loving human relationships.

Alpha is a community of adults and young adolescents who willingly learn, work, and live together in a harmonious climate driven by high expectations, initiative, individual choices, and remarkable degrees of responsibility and accountability well beyond what is even expected, much less accomplished through conventional school practices. The most direct way to learn what Alpha means is via the phenomenology of students' perceptions. They understand how it works for them and their classmates, and their testimonies are unequivocal; I know because I have interviewed generations of Alpha students over two decades. My university interns who have worked on the team find themselves changed forever. Strong communities are comprised of individuals who embrace commonly held beliefs, who function democratically, and who are bound by traditions they cherish. These principles are foundational in Alpha, and this manuscript teaches how naturally they have been and are still manifest.

While this volume is truly a history, it also stands as a written tribute to Carol Smith, Alpha's longest serving and most gifted teacher. For 25 years she remained doggedly focused on the goals, never losing sight of the urgency of matching schooling to the nature and needs of her students. It is also reassuring to note that since her retirement four years ago to consulting with other middle level educators, Alpha's current teachers and students have resolutely carried on. I have had intimate knowledge of this team for more than 20 years, and I am completely confident that the best of what has been achieved will continue. Alpha's teachers today are exquisitely clear in their understanding and vision and are gifted in their pedagogy; they will wisely and competently engage whatever challenges the day may present.

Middle level education has long needed access to this important story. Not only does it document the history of Alpha, but it reminds everyone—not just middle level educators—that the long term success of all education happens because (1) the program effectively accommodates the human nature and needs of the students and (2) teachers are savvy, responsive guardians of effective practice. While I suspect this lesson might be wasted on the three fellows who preached to me and each other about what "schools oughta be doing," it will ultimately carry the day with educators who are mindful of evidence and deeply committed to the continuing evolution of the middle level concept to best serve present and future generations of our nation's children.

Chris Stevenson
Professor Emeritus, University of Vermont
Pinehurst, North Carolina

September 2004

What Kids Say

Good Teachers...
are patient and understanding.
listen.
are friendly.
are clear and well organized.
are charismatic.
are creative and resourceful.
are knowledgeable.
are flexible and open-minded.
are fair.
like teaching and children.
keep on task.
relate well with others.
are good managers.
are risk-takers.
make learning exciting.
don't yell.
are trustworthy.
motivate students.
know how to find things out.
—Alpha Team Student Inquiry, 1992

What Parents Say

Good Teachers...
love children.
make learning fun.
listen, are open-minded, are innovative.
model good learning.
use parents as resources.
are honest.
are flexible.
have high standards.
communicate with others.
find the uniqueness in each child.
have a sense of humor.
are consistent.
are patient.
respect and explore differences.
integrate technology, literacy,
and numeracy.
—Alpha Parent Inquiry, 1992

The Story Behind the Story

Thinking back from this present time, which now has come to recognize the unique needs of children 10-14 years old, I find something poignant in my parent's decision to move before I entered sixth grade. This move caused me to switch schools, leaving Central School in the town where I grew up and enrolling in a school across the main highway that splits the town east and west. St. Johns is a small town, just 8,000 people, but it seemed to me as though I was entering a strange country with this change. Before the move I had already entered puberty and was feeling the "angst" most 10- to 14-year-old kids describe when they talk about their lives—unsettledness, tentativeness, self-consciousness, personal uniqueness. The move to the new school did little to lessen those feelings.

This move gave me a new perspective on schooling. At Central School I had gone about my days as a "busy active pupil" (at least that what was written on my report card), tending to do whatever activity caught my attention. The move to East Ward brought with it a different daily structure. Not only were all the kids new to me but so was the way the classroom operated. "Everydayness" here consisted of sitting in rows, hearing presentations, and performing number functions. All students worked on the same lesson, some bored because it was repetitive while others struggled. Once in awhile we would try to help each other, passing notes or whispering softly. Entering junior high also meant we switched classes. I never felt really comfortable in this environment and thought often about Central School and the happier days I had spent there. That is until seventh grade when I entered Mr. Griffin's social studies class.

I remember clearly sitting in Mr. Griffin's class. I was madly in love with him; and because he tilted his head to the side when he called on me, I was sure he secretly loved me too—although I talked to no one about this. One day he posed a question to the whole class—"What do you want to know about war?" I thought it a little strange, a teacher asking us what we wanted to know. He went up and down the rows soliciting responses. Most had questions about specific wars or sought information about heroes or weapons. When it was my turn I remember feeling color flush my face and a knot in the pit of my stomach. I felt uncomfortable making my own curiosity public. I didn't want to sound too "brainy." I could hardly get the words out of my mouth and was surprised at what I said. "I wonder," I offered in a raspy sort of voice, "why people fight." Thank goodness Mr. Griffin didn't ask me to explain; he just wrote my question on the board. I've marked that day in my memory as the time when I decided I wanted to partake in the intellectual life—one filled with exploration of thoughts and ideas. That one question in a seventh grade classroom started an inquiry that has formed my life ever since.

Remembered experiences like these were high moments and memorable ones, distanced from the ordinary and everyday. I realize now that the high moments were inroads into what I have come to regard as the best learning experiences for middle school students. These experiences captured what I researched and studied through graduate school and what I wanted for my children's education. They were the forerunners to what I came to value in the Alpha Program, a progressive, alternative program in Shelburne, Vermont.

This book chronicles the development of this unique educational adventure through its now 33 years of existence. My personal experiences with Alpha along with my preparation as an educational psychologist taught me to value the basic purposes of learning that were expressed in the program's establishment. The founders, in a letter to parents, set forth these five objectives for the program:

1. To train each child in the skills of responsibility and self-sufficiency.
2. To allow the child to take as much responsibility as can comfortably be handled, no more or less.
3. To do everything possible to ensure that most of the time, the child is happy and free of those outside pressures that really do not need to exist.

4. To lead the child to a form of self-discipline that will carry over to those situations where it will be the only discipline worth having.
5. To encourage the formation of an intellectually curious and creative being, well grounded in basic knowledge and ready to apply it to a field of learning far beyond the usual.

These objectives remind me of the feelings I had as a young adolescent in that Midwestern town trying to understand myself and the world around me—the feeling of not being in control but when given some liberty, the wonderful sense of adventure; the feeling of being limited by curricular parameters but when given the freedom to explore, finding an insatiable curiosity; the feeling of satisfaction when teachers, who hold a good deal of knowledge, tapped into my interests; the warm, opening up feeling of being cared about; and a recognition that one teacher can make a difference in the life of a young adolescent.

Although these five goals of Alpha were ideals, they were made manifest over the three decades of the program's existence. What began as principles became practices and procedures. Because of their importance as foundations and continuing guides I have organized the chapters by these five goals, indicating, at least to me, how the Alpha program moved into its "own skin" as the years went by and various problems were encountered.

John Dewey emphasized the concept that education is a form of social life. In school, as in life generally, one's personal history, the traditions of which one is a part, and the social and community relations in which one engages, outline day to day life. Narrative inquiry is a way of translating Dewey's conception into a practical method of research and is the technique I employed in conducting this project. This book is largely a retelling of the educational experiences of those involved in Alpha, not necessarily in chronological order. The stories reflect the world of Alpha as I have seen it from the worlds I inhabit. I used observations and interviews; data from field notes, interview transcripts, and a whole array of non-storied, written material such as newsletters, records, rules, pictures, and official statements. Because I was living in Shelburne 33 years ago, and my oldest son started fourth grade in 1975, I had the good fortune of being able to watch up close as Alpha developed and adapted to various pressures.

I offer here the findings of one who has tried to glean insight from students' experiences and teachers' recollections as well as from my own direct participation. The Alpha story is one that needs to be told widely, and its messages contemplated seriously by middle level educators. The remarkable success of this multiage, genuinely student-centered educational community, wherein the curriculum is integrated, well-documented in this volume, should give heart to those who want to make the education of young adolescents all that it needs to be and can be. Are we willing to listen to Alpha students? Are we willing to invest in procedures students identify as crucial to their learning? The answers could shape the middle school agenda for the coming years. 🏃

The author, Susan Kuntz, interviewing Alpha students Brad Kraushaar and Stuart Hayes.

I

The Beginning

1. To train each child in the skills of responsibility and self-sufficiency. —First objective of program, adopted 1971

Shelburne Village is located along the Eastern banks of Lake Champlain in the foothills of the Green Mountains of Vermont. Governor Benning Wentworth of New Hampshire granted the village a charter in 1763. During the early years of its founding, the village consisted of a series of small dairy farms and a few merchants who settled around the town green. A general store, town hall, and village school were constructed in the last half of the 19th century. Gradually, as in most New England settlements, the green became the place of gathering as shops and businesses opened to provide services to a growing population.

The population of the village increased substantially in the 1960s. Urban sprawl from Burlington, Vermont's largest city, spilled over to the village to its south. People migrated to Vermont from other places during these years and mainly settled in Shelburne. Some sought escape from larger metropolitan areas in New England such as Boston or Hartford; others ventured East from the Midwest looking for new adventure and a sense of community thought to exist in small New England towns.

Today, Shelburne consists of a mixture of residential homes mostly of people who work in Burlington, the city 10 miles north, and a cluster of local businesses in the historic village green area. Its geographic region from north to south runs along Route 7 paralleling

the lake. Land to the east of the Route 7 passageway is largely rural residential with a few dairy farms Much of the land between Route 7 and the lake, including large stretches of shoreline, has been preserved in large parcels of land holdings assembled around the turn of the century by the Webb family.

Sitting back from the road between the 18th Century Shelburne Museum and the 1440-acre estate of the Webb family is the Community School. Constructed in 1967, it was the first middle school in Vermont. According to John Winton, the original principal, the middle school concept was "in the wind" during this time; and when the growing population in Shelburne indicated a new school was needed, the board of directors recommended a separate school to accommodate youth ages 10-14.

There was some controversy in the community about the decision at that time. A consolidated high school had opened two years previously taking older students from the town's one village school to another community for their education. Long time citizens of Shelburne favored the idea of a town school that held all 12 grades in one building. Splitting Shelburne students between three schools seemed impractical and strange to these residents who had spent all of their own school days in one building. They liked the idea of all their children attending the same school; it seemed simpler and less complicated. An older sibling could accompany younger ones to school, and parents would only have to deal with one administrative structure. These citizens took seriously their responsibility for educating their youth and felt there was more local control when students stayed in Shelburne in one building.

On the other side were citizens who advocated a school organization that supported developmental levels of students, a concept proposed by Vermont native John Dewey fifty years before and popularized by many educational researchers at this time. Appropriate education, these more progressive citizens maintained, should be in harmony with knowledge about the growth and development of children within an age span. They supported three groups of schooling corresponding to typical developmental levels outlined in literature—elementary, middle, and high school. They believed that children who are in developmentally appropriate situations are likely to be less stressed and more motivated. They would have better work habits, be more creative, and demonstrate better skills than children in developmentally inappropriate circumstances. They pointed out that during the childhood years, the classroom was the major context for the performance of the child. As children moved into the middle years between 10 and 14, the school environment would increase in scope and complexity as the functioning of the child changed because of maturity. Looking at student-school interaction in this way gave a different perspective on how to organize educational settings. The fundamental point made by developmentalists was that an appropriate school organization is essential to the healthy development of students. They included identity development along with intellectual development as reasons to have separate programs and buildings arguing that social-emotional levels are enhanced as students learn suitable standards of right and wrong and understand how conceptions of a social system function by interacting with peers.

> *After widespread debate, a community survey indicated support for the construction of a new building for those "students in the middle."*

Looking at student stages of maturity and matching them with an educational setting was an approach that had not been a consideration when all grades were in one village school. But with growing numbers of pupils to accommodate in Shelburne, the wise solution, it seemed, was to provide distinct configurations of grades and separate buildings.

After widespread discussion and debate, a community survey indicated support for the construction of a new school building for those "students in the middle." John Winton moved from Massachusetts to become the principal and oversee the construction of the building. He remembers "the middle school concept hadn't really caught on yet," but it was being implemented in other states—a few in New England although none in Vermont. The idea in Shelburne originated with Barbara Snelling, the school board chair at the time. Winton recalls the day school opened. "The building was full of workmen. As they completed one wing, all grades moved into that one area. As we gained pieces of the building, the school spread out." He told me that in hindsight he realizes "what an advantage we had then." Community members gave him latitude to arrange the building as he wanted. This flexibility served the configuration of the middle level concept well. He said "everybody expected the school to be different; therefore, anything done was sort of taken philosophically as "it's a middle school and that's what the middle school is." Winton's colleagues in neighboring towns, principals of traditional junior high schools, didn't give him much support; in fact, he says they gave him a lot of grief, making comments about the unusual nature and organization of the Shelburne school. He didn't listen to them because their buildings were little high schools in scheduling and philosophy—large, complex, and impersonal. The middle school movement, as he had come to know it, argued that junior high schools were not meeting the needs of youth 10 to 14 years of age, and educators who believed in developmentally appropriate organizations fought for a design that reflects characteristics of young adolescents. In recent decades several indicators of growth and development during early adolescence, one being the early onset of puberty, had been identified and called for a new approach to educating this age group. John said the idea that the new school in Shelburne would be "focused around what was happening with kids around that time in their lives" was fascinating.

The move of grades 4-8 to the new building allowed the teachers and administrators in the Village School to look at different configurations for their classrooms as well. Additional space prompted teachers and administrators to consider alternative curricular options for the primary grades. Some embraced a move toward a "progressive" view of education in keeping with the "open classroom movement" still popular in the 1960s. Mostly this meant providing flexible space so students could move around freely and engage in activities that involved individual and small-group instruction. Faculty, who had been newly hired to accommodate an increasing student population, had studied in teacher preparation programs that emphasized newer curricular dimensions and spoke in favor of using developmental stages to plan programs.

Emergence of an alternative approach

In order to address the curricular tension felt in the community, teachers, board representatives, and community members in Shelburne and its neighboring village, Charlotte, joined together during the 1968-69 school year to study "alternative" approaches to educating their youth, ones that would provide the best education for all the children. The School Directors of Shelburne established a Project Board. Various members of this board told me they remember spending time reading about, discussing, and visiting programs built on the open classroom idea.

Defining education as "open" worried many parents and community members. They were concerned about what appeared to be lack of structure and a "watering down of content." They wanted an educational environment they understood, where students went to classes to study single subjects, sat in desks behind closed doors, and where bells delineated the beginning and ending of periods. Some were leery of having students spend large parts of the day working on projects together. They didn't know what to think about emphasizing children's social and emotional development in school or having teachers work with other teachers in the same classroom.

The Project Board sought assistance with designing a K-8 curriculum from an outside professional educator, Marian Stroud, who had recently moved to Vermont. Marian came with experience from the English system of open education and had directed a federally funded project to bring innovative educational techniques to central Vermont schools. Mrs. Stroud conducted workshops for teachers and community members to explain the philosophy and characteristics of a new way of designing learning experiences, featuring multigrade classrooms and individual pupil instruction. After much study and discussion, the school boards in Shelburne and Charlotte decided that alternative programs that favored a team

The school boards decided that alternative programs that favored a team approach to teaching and a multilevel approach to learning would be an option in grades K-4.

approach to teaching and a multilevel approach to learning would be an option in grades K-4 for families who desired it in the 1970 school year. Parents could choose to have their children in a traditional single grade, single teacher classroom; or they could choose the new alternative setting where students had access to multiple teachers and space. Providing options seemed an obvious way to ease the tension between the proponents of both sides. With this decision the concept of choice became a part of the fabric of the Shelburne school community that survived through the years. The notion of an alternative approach to education also became a permanent part of the curricular offerings. These two ideas underlie a series of conflicts and tensions that have permeated schooling in Shelburne ever since.

> *Parents could choose to have their children in a traditional single grade, single teacher classroom; or they could choose the new alternative setting where students had access to multiple teachers and space.*

Considerable recognition was given to Shelburne for its decision to offer curricular options. A national newspaper, *The Christian Science Monitor,* ran a story on the idea of options within the school. This article described the difficulties and benefits of offering "real options" within a public school emphasizing the compromise that was necessary for such an endeavor. One representative of the original committee was quoted as saying it took an exorbitant amount of time to design an alternative project because it meant, "negotiating with everyone from principals to parents to pupils."

Realizing that staffing was critical for the success of the new program, the Project Board suggested that teachers from the existing staff be recruited to teach in the program and that instructional aides be hired to assist in each room, a policy unheard of at the time. Along with aides, teachers recruited a host of parent volunteers. "Everyone felt involved in the process," says the school board chair at the time. Part of the commitment to the program by families was parent involvement in the classroom. Along with parents, community members were recruited to share particular talents or interests with the class. "There's a lot of community education involved in a project like this, and I'd like to see community involvement expand," remarked one parent aide to the reporter of the *Christian Science Monitor*. Involving parents and community members intricately in the classroom helped get recognition and acceptance for the new programs in the broader village community. The Village School principal told me the Project Board continued to be active after the decision had been made to institute these programs. He says they wrote grants and administered federal and state funds awarded to innovative projects; they even supervised the collection of classroom materials that ranged from "wood scraps to used buttons."

From the beginning, this board was interested in determining how the "alternative" approach to education affected student learning and so they set up an elaborate evaluation system. While they certainly were interested in obtaining performance scores for all school programs, they particularly targeted the multiage classrooms as an area of study. They hired a professional evaluation consultant to review the project. A Project Board member told me, "…we wanted to measure not only reading, writing, and arithmetic, but other things too, like self-concept and self-confidence, that were important to us." The results after the first year indicated that children in the open, multigrade classrooms performed equal to, or ahead of, their peers in areas of basic skills. The alternative curricular project was declared a resounding success at the primary level.

> *The alternative curricular project*
> *was declared a resounding success*
> *at the primary level.*

A school for the "middle"

Despite the arguments made for developmental structures for students 10-14 and even though the primary grades offered curricular options, the newly constructed middle school opened its first year, 1968-69, with single grade classrooms for grades 4-8. Curricular offerings in the sixth through eighth grades were flexible but still within the confines of content specific classrooms. Although the building had been constructed with partial walls separating individual rooms, curricular structures resembled those descriptive of junior high schools across the country. Individual grade levels were physically separated from each other with the fourth and fifth grades self-contained and the sixth through eighth grade students transitioning between subject-area classrooms. Students in the upper grades noticed some changes in their learning environment. They had to adjust from a small, contained classroom structure to a larger more flexible school structure; going from one teacher to three; and they learned to interact with a more heterogeneous set of peers. There was also increased focus on achievement and performance as they progressed from the fourth and fifth grades to the sixth, seventh, and eighth grades. Although the new school had been built with the developmental needs of the children in mind, the daily activities did not correspond fully with these needs. The fourth and fifth grades were typical of those classrooms found anywhere where specific time was allotted to reading, math, spelling, and other areas. Students sat at desks or tables and used textbooks or workbooks to follow along with their lessons. Occasionally, however, projects were done with the whole class involved in a study of a particular topic. In the upper grades (6-8), social studies, science, math, language arts, were taught during different periods. Students transitioned between classrooms as assigned.

A building had been constructed to house middle school students and was a public recognition of this developmental age, a transition from childhood to adolescence. The structure was in place and the educational conversation shifted to one that considered how academic and social-emotional patterns of development might be interwoven for this age. The task that occupied teachers and community members in Shelburne for the next two decades was how that interplay would be reflected in the curriculum.

"The Nameless Idea" is born

During the second year of the middle school's existence, 1970-71, a teacher, Jim Reid, wanted to do things differently in his fourth grade classroom. Initially, he requested permission to remove some of the structures to learning found in the traditional classroom setting. He wanted students to be able to set their own goals for learning and determine a timeline within the week for completing them. When he spoke about his idea to others in the school he talked about the various models of education debated in the public sphere implied in the questions posed decades ago by John Dewey.

Can students operate without firm guidance from others and be self-reliant and self-motivated? Do teachers need to plan students' time or can students plan its use? To parents, other teachers, and the administrators Jim posed the question that formed the basis of his teaching philosophy—can we trust students to make responsible choices about how they spend their time? He believed we could and proposed a program that gave students the responsibility for organizing their week. In his plan students would complete a goal sheet each morning where they would list the subject areas in which they would be working that day and the time they would spend doing so. Students could work individually or in small groups on their assignments. Jim knew the person most likely to be in a position to shape the organizational conditions necessary for success was the principal and so he talked with him about his thinking. "I don't exactly know what I'm doing yet, but I've been doing a lot of reading, and there are just some things I'd like to do with kids, try to give them a little more responsibility." John, the principal, said, "Try it, if we run into problems we'll back off; but go ahead."

The question was raised—can we trust
students to make responsible choices
about how they spend their time?

Jim also discussed his idea with colleagues and parents. While many parents today may be familiar with the concepts of students setting their own goals and individualized learning plans, it was a new idea in 1970 especially for a public school setting. Jim set up his classroom with tables instead of desks to accommodate the flexibility needed for the program. He began teaching students how to take responsibility for their own time by providing a list of the activities they needed to accomplish during the week. On his desk he kept a folder for each student where weekly time sheets were kept. John Winton told me he visited the room often to see what was going on. Jim would work with the kids at the beginning of the week and determine what it is they were to accomplish for the week. They would set that down on paper, and Jim would hold them to it. By the end of the week, they had to have met their obligations.

John said after his visits he was "enthusiastic" about what he saw and so were the parents because "the kids liked it." The program was called "self-selection" to signify its premise. John said he kept an eye on the program during the first year and was impressed by how "a single teacher changed the nature of learning for students in his class." He supported the efforts of Jim because there were exciting things happening in this classroom, but he also remained watchful about the effects on the students and the rest of the school.

There was a general understanding between the administration of the school and Jim that he could proceed with his idea as long as it didn't cause problems and as long as he "functioned within the overall context of the school and its schedule." Jim was careful to define learning expectations for the class that correlated with the fourth-grade curricular goals set by the school. Given the parameters set forth in the curriculum guide, students would then determine how and when they would accomplish them. This aspect of responsibility when given to students also changed the role of the teacher. What might now seem like a minor adjustment in the daily classroom structure, got at the core of the learning process for Jim. He explained the educational purpose of this adjustment in a newsletter to parents soliciting their support. He explained that their children would be working on their own as soon as possible and at times would be expected to plan and complete work independently. Initially, parents went along with this change in classroom structure because their children were excited about going to school. Although there were certainly trying moments in the development of this process, Jim told me that "the most important outcome of the first year was that students succeeded." When I asked him what this meant, he said, "Students learned the material they would have in a more traditional classroom and they also learned how to study it themselves." The principal and the parents gave approval because they saw that students weren't "harmed" by the removal of some institutional structures such as textbooks and set class periods. So "Self-Selection" began a second year.

When placing students in classrooms for the next fall, the principal encouraged expansion of the program because there was enough student and parent interest to warrant it. Barbara Macamer, a recently hired fourth grade teacher with a classroom right next to Jim's, accepted the invitation to join the effort, and they designed a curriculum that involved both of their classrooms.

Since the classrooms were side-by-side, students moved easily between them for activities. In both rooms students set their own goals and established time frames for carrying them out. Jim and Barbara began planning together allowing students to group across classrooms for activities. In actuality, they became the first teaching team in Shelburne Middle School, a practice that was becoming popular among middle schools nationally. Jim had not originally considered offering "Self-Selection" as a teaming endeavor but saw the benefits of it when watching Barbara teach. He admitted he had resisted the idea of teaming when suggested by John but said "the more I saw what Barbara was doing and the more she saw what I was doing it seemed to make sense." Jim told me after they finally got together, they decided to ask John if they could team the following year. He says, "we figured out later that, of course, that's what John had in mind all along." This second year was one of trials and errors. Looking back on it now, Jim said "we made a lot of mistakes...we backed off and went down another corridor that looked like it would be better; then we charged ahead. For the most part it worked; we just did it."

> ### *Jim and Barbara became the first teaching team in Shelburne Middle School.*

During this year, Jim and Barbara learned to work closely together using each other as sounding boards for ideas, picking one another up after a failed activity attempt, talking together about student progress and innovative ideas, all the areas written about by educational researchers a decade later when teaming became popular. When it was time to organize student loads and classrooms for the 1972 school year, they decided to combine their two classrooms and give the program a name, something that would catch the tone of the ideas they wanted to present. They called it "The Nameless Idea." In a newsletter to parents they explained the name as follows:

> *It probably seems a little odd to call anything The Nameless Idea, but we did it with a purpose. Terms like open classroom, continuous progress, and others can in reality stand for hundreds of different ways of achieving the same goals. We are honestly afraid that the use of any name in particular will freeze a definite picture of the class in each mind, and that the picture*

probably won't be the same from one mind to the next.
We are concerned also that presenting what we do as a
package will prevent us from making changes in it that
might improve the approach. We like the freedom of
being able to steal whatever is good from whereever we
happen to find it.

They chose the name because they knew the program would evolve and didn't want it labeled by some existing perception. They wanted to be able to maneuver the program as it developed; making it fit the students they encountered. Although in theory their idea of maintaining flexibility was a good one in the years to come, it became a problem as some citizens called for accountability and judged the worth of the program from their own educational standpoints.

During the early years students responded positively to the changes made in these fourth grade classrooms. One alumnus of the program told me that this classroom built for her a sense of competence and self understanding. She said she "learned the skill of using time effectively so that in the long run I would meet the goals I had set earlier." Another former student said creating the schedule was not the hardest part of the process but creating goals for herself that were challenging yet obtainable was the most difficult skill to grasp. This was precisely what Jim and Barbara had in mind when they gave students responsibilities. This same graduate told me that she learned through the process to identify her "own abilities to accomplish work and her capabilities and limitations as a learner." I think this is exactly the self-understanding John Dewey had in mind a half century earlier in the readings Jim devoured.

> ## *Goal setting and time management as student responsibilities gave this program a unique delineation that set it apart from other classrooms in Shelburne for the next 33 years.*

Goal setting and time management as student responsibilities gave this program a unique delineation that set it apart from other classrooms in the Shelburne School for the next 33 years. Students who were a part of this and subsequent classes said that the organizing skills learned in the The Nameless Idea carried into their future lives. These "habits of practice," as they were labeled in stories told to me, benefitted them throughout their lives. Years later, after they had left the middle school, graduates tell me they attribute their good organizational skills to "making my own schedule each day"..."learning how to manage my time wisely"... "writing each day's schedule on paper to help guide me through." One alumnus attributes success in his current position to learning how to see the "big picture and prioritize activities." He said his experience in this program instilled in him the ability to handle many different tasks.

Jim and Barbara had created an educational program with The Nameless Idea that met many of the developmental needs of young adolescents by allowing flexibility in their learning activities. And it was exciting for students. The coming decades would see the development and solidification of a program philosophy that expanded student responsibility in the classroom by allowing them to determine what was to be learned as well as the time needed to learn it. This change did not happen without disagreement from parts of the school and community or without some tension from within the program itself. The next twenty years, 1970s and 80s, were ones of introspection and clarification for those involved in the alternative program. It was a period during which characteristics of the program were articulated and parameters for the alternative nature were defined. 🏃

II
Expansion and Definition

2. To allow the child to take as much responsibility as can comfortably be handled—no more or less.
        —Second objective of program, adopted 1971

Parents of children who were in the The Nameless Idea program for the first two years were pleased with the learning that was happening in these fourth grade rooms where their children were doing "interesting" things. They resisted having their children leave for a traditional fifth grade class the next year. A few of them talked to Jim and Barbara about making it a two-year program, keeping the fourth grade students for an additional year as the students became fifth graders and adding a new group of fourth graders. Jim told me he had been doing a good deal of reading about middle school organization that showed there is a great variety in individual levels of cognitive and social development during the early adolescent years and that transitional changes to a different class each year can be stressful to them because they happen simultaneously with other more personal changes, those associated with puberty. Most research he had read supported multiyear classrooms indicating adolescents are ready to take on increased responsibility and independence at the same time as they decrease dependence on parents. He also noted that there is the emergence of at least some aspects of abstract thought during the ages between 10 and 14. However, the onset of such changes vary tremendously with individual students. Jim felt what was needed to accommodate the varying demands of these students was a classroom that minimized some school organizational factors that work against developmental growth. Because Jim's interest was in aligning philosophical understandings with structural goals, he proposed to the administration a multiyear program that included students from fourth through eighth grade. Although this idea was new at the middle level, at the primary level multilevel classrooms in Shelburne provided a model. Since the idea of multiage classrooms was emerging nationally, the principal supported Jim's idea to try a multigraded program. A small number of students in fourth to eighth grade were recruited for the first year. Barbara stayed with the self-contained fourth grade, and a new teacher was assigned to work with Jim. Her perspective on the endeavor proved to differ greatly from Jim's, and she was reassigned after one year. During the 1974-75 school year Warren, who had watched the classroom begin while student teaching in Shelburne the year before, joined Jim as part of the teaching team. Warren had been a scout leader for many years and was interested in academic activities that happened outside of the classroom, particularly those that combined nature studies with educational ones. Philosophically, his interests matched Jim's intent for the multigraded classroom. There was no difficulty in filling the class with students, especially fourth and fifth graders, and a few seventh and eighth graders joined who were adventuresome and intrigued by the idea of doing something new.

Parents were attracted by the idea of the multiyear nature of the classroom. It created opportunities for restructuring the curriculum and student activities. Their children no longer would transition from a small, contained classroom structure to a larger one as they advanced in grade. Nor would they have to change teachers during the five years. All students would remain with a small group of classmates during their time in the program allowing them to know each other well, a factor thought important to the social and intellectual development of students of this age. Small groupings would allow students to work together.

The change in structure also prompted a change in name for the class. In the principal's office one day while discussing with Jim the program's expansion and how to explain it to outside constituencies, John suggested we give the program a name that didn't mean anything...like Alpha. It came as simply as that. "Alpha" seemed appropriate because it was a name that did not identify it with the often criticized open classroom movement ("progressive" and "new-school" were ruled out). The name "Alpha" seemed harmless yet novel enough to solicit query from potential students; it is the name that remains in use today.

The teachers developed a statement of educational purpose as the foundation for the organizational structure of the classroom that embraced the principles of learning proclaimed by middle level educators at that time. The 1974-75 Handbook of Alpha stated

> At a minimum, education should equip a student to read, write, and express him or herself as well as possible; to be able to do numerical calculations in order to conduct household affairs; and to have an acquaintance with the world geography, its social and political makeup, and its history. But most importantly, a full education must teach the value of curiosity and unaverage thinking. It must introduce and develop methodical and efficient ways to learn; always operating on the supposition that a human who knows how to learn, and to love doing it, has an advantage in life. A full education includes the appreciation of beauty and humor in the world, abilities that not only define a human as human, but that help to preserve one's sanity and perspective.

This statement made it clear that this classroom would emphasize more than the usual subject area content (the "what" of learning); it would include the development of strategies, skills, and dispositions (the "hows and whys" of learning). This statement became the standard for making programmatic decisions over the 33 years of the program's existence. The underlying notion of those involved

> *The underlying notion in Alpha was that students would be active in their learning, determining not only what was to be studied but also how to go about it.*

in Alpha was that students would be active in their learning, determining not only what was to be studied but also how to go about it. Teachers structured the classroom environment to invite inquiry and participation by students in all areas of the curriculum.

Program expansion

Student interest in the Alpha Program grew steadily from 1973 to 1976, prompted, in part, by media attention to the needs of young adolescents. With growing demand for placement in the program, an additional teacher, Carol Smith, was added to the Alpha Team in 1975. Carol had taught in an adjacent town before coming to Shelburne to teach fourth grade in 1974. John Winton asked her to look at the alternative program as it was developing. She admits that she was terrified at first of the responsibility, the uniqueness, the organization; but she was also intrigued by the opportunity. She decided to join the team of the multiage class primarily because she was "caught by the excitement." The philosophy fit her beliefs about the place of schools in meeting adolescent needs—creating environments that were positive for social and emotional growth. She said she always thought schools should be willing and able to adapt practices to meet the individual differences of students. She saw that possibility in Alpha. One of the goals of the program that appealed to her as outlined in the handbook statement was to make learning "meaningful." She interpreted this to mean that student needs and desires should fit with curricular content and activities.

Carol's addition at this time was instrumental to defining the curriculum and proved pivotal for the direction of the program in future years, for she became the cornerstone of the Alpha vision for the next 25 years. She remains the teacher associated most closely with Alpha today and is the teacher spoken about most often by alumni years later. One graduate told me Carol was the reason she chose Alpha.

> I looked into the regular program before entering 7th and 8th grade. I was torn. I ultimately chose Alpha. My reason, Carol Smith. She was amazing. She could see what I was agonizing with but always let me make my own decisions. I adored Carol, because she seemed to really care for my well being. I didn't seem as just another student. She made everyone feel special.

Carol's presence on the teaching team strengthened the student development focus in the classroom. Her interest in the social and emotional needs of young adolescents, Jim's emphasis on philosophical and organizational notions, and Warren's interest in activity-based learning made the Alpha team of teachers complete. As they worked together to develop and refine aspects of the program, they established a close relationship and shared academic, social, and personal needs for many years. They told me they felt as if together they "were always on a mission."

Specific physical space was set aside in the building for Alpha. This space was comprised of three traditionally sized classrooms. Sliding doors could be opened or closed; project areas were designated; quiet space was designed; students and teachers moved about the space freely. Because they occupied one wing of the school Alpha was relatively isolated. They received the same funding opportunities as other established classrooms but no additional funds for student or teacher initiatives in the new program, no staff development that might help teachers and classroom aides understand individualized learning or multiage groupings—and no common planning time for the teachers!

The Alpha Team, 1976, Grades 4-8

Teachers: Carol Smith, upper left hand corner. Jim Reid, upper right hand corner, and Warren Steadman, partially hidden under Jim Reid.

Program definition

The years from 1975 into the early 1980s were times of definition as well as expansion for the Alpha Program. Teachers along with students and parents met regularly to determine how the

19

program philosophy was to be carried out in daily activities. Parent groups focused on clarifying and explaining the Alpha mission while teachers and students explored possibilities for curriculum. The course of study was constructed around ideas associated with an "integrated day," a concept which had to do with flexible time and variable order for learning. Perhaps Marion Stroud's visit to Shelburne in the late 1960s to present the British primary structure had familiarized people in the community with the "integrated day" concept; so people were not opposed to the concept that more than a decade later was introduced as Alpha.

The main difficulty with implementing an "integrated day" in the middle school in Shelburne was the challenge of scheduling. In fact, the concept offered the first curricular debate, separating Alpha from the rest of the school. In Alpha, Jim, Warren, and Carol with one instructional aide organized, planned, implemented, and assessed the learning experiences in all disciplines for 60 students from five grade levels. The co-curricular "specials" such as physical education and art were incorporated into the regular class day by the teachers of Alpha, unlike other rooms in the school where students were pulled out by grade level to work with specialty teachers. According to the principal, this was a compromise that had more to do with philosophy than schedule. He told me "if Alpha sent students by grade level to the specials, some would almost always be absent from the classroom during the day; and that condition would seriously damage the kind of community learning and group time needed in an integrated program."

Carol told me teachers felt this arrangement was not only a question of program philosophy but one of administrative inflexibility with regard to an already determined schedule. The mixed age group of Alpha did not fit with the grade level groupings on the master schedule for specialty teachers. Alpha teachers felt the issue was not that the specialty teachers objected to changing the groupings, although some of them did, but that the fixed schedule determined how specials were arranged. In their view the schedule dictated the practice.

The result of this conflict was that during most of the early years teachers in Alpha planned and provided for the specials on their own—one teaching physical education, another teaching music and art. Sometimes a kindly art or music teacher would visit to assist with a project or activity, but these occurrences were rare. The Alpha classroom became a world of its own, completely self-sufficient as far as curricular and co-curricular activities were concerned. Carol Smith told me that during this time "we always said we could slice our little wing off of the building and throw it out to sea, and nobody would miss us, and we could be fine." The advantage to this isolation was that they could try things, take risks, but underneath these attempts they knew their limit—anything is okay as long as it doesn't affect the rest of the school. The functional structures of Alpha were established during the decade of the 1970s; students set their own schedules, teachers presented general goals and monitored student progress; time and order of learning were variable. The organizational arrangement that evolved during those years set Alpha apart and continues to be a distinctive feature today.

Multiage grouping

Multiage is a term commonly used to describe mixed-age groups when two or more grade levels have been intentionally blended together in the belief that students' learning and growth will be improved. Students are able to interact across age groups and have long-term relationships with other students and teachers, both shown to have positive effects on performance and achievement.

> *The multiage aspect of Alpha was an ideal opportunity for curricular integration involving all ages and developmental levels*

The multiage aspect of Alpha was an ideal opportunity for curricular integration involving all ages and developmental levels. Teachers felt it was natural to align curriculum with needs of students. The range of ages (from 9-14) and grade-levels (5) in the class encouraged a variety of activities at numerous levels and gave students flexibility in finding a place to comfortably work. They had the opportunity to move from the top in one area of study to a lower one in another.

In a multiage program, students of different ages learn side-by-side. Older students who otherwise might not assume leadership roles now have the opportunity to become leaders. One student told me that it was the multiage aspect that increased her opinion of her own abilities. She said that her favorite part of Alpha was the way it allowed her to grow into a leader. "I don't think I would have had the chance if I had been in regular. I was a shy person when I came into fourth grade, but by the time I left, the younger kids described me on my goodbye card as outgoing, take-charge, and leader-of-the-pack." Other students told me that the multiyear experience helped them gain skills in leadership, observation, collaboration, compromise, goal setting, and decision making. Over the years students were given time to grow into leadership roles. One student told me that during her first two years in Alpha she was "just one of the students," but her confidence grew and as she "became more involved with class decisions" she took on leadership in class governance moving from secretary to treasurer and finally to moderator. Developing leadership skills helped adolescents with overall adjustment and increased self-esteem. Having the opportunity to move in and out of leadership roles in the classroom increased student confidence levels and encouraged the development of appropriate decision-making skills. Students reported that when they took on these class roles they felt quite "grown up" and didn't get stuck in the top-dog-bottom-dog phenomenon of power relations. One important aspect of this issue that I heard from stories told me is that people are not necessarily born leaders but develop the skills gradually. Many students believed that spending several years with one group of peers gave them the opportunity to acquire and expand leadership skills.

Research studies provide limited findings on the effects of multiage and multigrade groupings. Ansab (1989) found that some children benefit from multigrade classes while others do better in single grade classes. He also noted findings that suggest multigrade grouping does tend to be associated with better self-concept and attitude toward school. A Canadian study conducted by Brown and Martin (1989) noted no differences in achievement between students in a multiage setting and their matched counterparts in single grade classrooms. Gutierrez and Slavin (1992), Pavan (1992), and Miller (1990) found that children in non-graded multilevel classrooms fare as well or better than children in single graded classrooms on standardized measure of achievement.

The greatest advantages for students in multiage settings that I found in my observations and conversation with students in Alpha are in the areas of social and emotional competence. Multigraded classrooms provide a wide range of behaviors for students to fit into.

Student stories indicated that they learned to feel comfortable with themselves and over the years came to understand and appreciate their own way of learning. Having various age and levels of achievement in one classroom encouraged students to reach beyond what might be expected of them.

Many graduates of the Alpha Program told me that the multiage feature of Alpha permitted them to fit where they were suited, socially and academically. What was expected from them was what they were ready and able to do. One graduate who through his years in Alpha did work typical of an older student (algebra in 5th grade) told me he appreciated not being labeled "advanced or gifted," a designation that would have marked him as a nerd in other classrooms. The flexibility in this class gave him opportunities to work with a small group of students doing algebraic expressions. It seemed easy and natural. Another student told of her struggles with computational facts through most of the four years; but she never felt as if she were behind, and by the end of eighth grade she could do the math required to advance to high school.

Teachers in Alpha did not assume that possessing some knowledge was expected because of one's age or grade level; rather, students, along with teachers, figured out what they needed to know, put it into their weekly goals, and went about learning it. This was not to say that there were not expectations in knowledge and skill areas. When I asked students how they knew what areas to work on they said they learned quickly that the mastery of some concepts and skills was needed before they could meet their goals for the week. The practice in Alpha, as I came to understand this part of it, was that curriculum standards were met when it seemed reasonable to do so. Reasonableness, however, depended on student readiness and willingness. The multiyear aspect of Alpha permitted flexibility in meeting those standards.

Alpha teachers believe that adolescents are motivated to discover the underlying meaning of things as part of the effort to make sense out of their world.

23

The range of academic behaviors demonstrated by students in Alpha also promoted the idea of individualized learning. Alpha teachers believe that adolescents are motivated to discover the underlying meaning of things as part of the effort to make sense out of their world. Teachers then aid with this discovery by helping students explore, talk about, and process their environments. On my visits to Alpha I often saw teachers talking to students about their performance, offering suggestions, and saying such things as "You are ready to move along; why don't you join this group"? or "This may take a very long time, you may want to get more help." It was evident that students were actively involved in discussing their own learning with teachers and in assessing their pace in completing goals. Each student had a plan. Parents were impressed with the way their children talked about their learning, emphasizing the skills and knowledge mastered. One parent told me she liked "the idea that kids examined what they're learning, why they're learning it, and how they're learning it." She thought the whole process was "marvelous." The concept underlying individualized learning is that all students can learn but do so at different rates and in various ways; and they can help one another.

> *Parents were impressed with the way their children talked about their learning...the whole process was "marvelous."*

Multiage groupings helped Alpha students foster the skills needed to work with others. Working together brought different backgrounds, experiences, and skills to the learning activity. Students saw the concept or issue being studied through numerous lens. These multiple perspectives enriched discussions and the processes involved in learning. Students discovered how to motivate others through gentle encouragement and example. One student described her experience working with a group in these statements:

> *Alpha taught me how to be a productive member of a group whether I was a leader or just a participant. That skill is important for the "real world" because I know that when I get a job I will need to work*

well with others...It was frustrating for me to deal with the unmotivated members. I knew that if I got angry at them, they would become less productive and eventually give up; I had seen it happen before. I decided to work with them, be encouraging, and help them get motivated about the project and eventually most of them became contributing members of our group.

The multiage setting of Alpha was a factor in developing a learning atmosphere where younger students learn from older ones who, in turn, built their own skills by practicing and teaching what they knew. In the classroom I saw older students guiding younger ones in planning schedules and structuring activities. I noticed how confidence in their own abilities grew as they helped classmates, and I saw the look of self-assurance on their faces as they demonstrated competence. Younger students were paired with older ones as "learning goal partners" at the beginning of the year. These pairs met together each week reviewing progress toward goals set the previous week and setting new ones for the week ahead. I heard them talking about how to accomplish work and establish realistic expectations. When I asked one student about how she knew what goals to set for herself she described for me the importance of having a goal partner to guide her, especially when she was new to the program. She said:

I remember my first day of fourth grade in Alpha, scared and surrounded by a sea of new faces. I was asked to plan my first day's schedule, set a week's worth of goals for myself, and design a project. I was overwhelmed. Luckily, an eighth grader, my guardian angel, was assigned to help me. She knew how to schedule her time so that she could accomplish her goals; her goals were challenging, yet obtainable; she knew how to design great projects and she was confident in herself. She got me through the harrowing first days of fourth grade. As I look back upon my Alpha experience, I knew the most important thing was that I became a mature, confident eighth grader. Alpha taught me how to work with others and be a self-motivated learner. It also taught me the important skills of responsibility and leadership.

The original five-year span of time spent in Alpha gave students many opportunities to develop and grow in areas that built confidence in their abilities. They had time to practice and time to lead. They learned to value their contributions to the class.

In my visits, the variety of groupings used for discussions and projects was notable; students were grouped and regrouped by teachers as well as given the opportunity to group themselves. This flexibility seemed to address diverse student needs, interests, and learning goals at particular points in time. The multiage, multiyear structure supported continuing relationships between students and teachers who acted as constants in each other's lives. Alpha became a community of learners across ages, interests, and viewpoints. One of the great discoveries this multiyear experience provides for adults is, as an instructional aide told me, that it is "Okay to sit back and let kids be where they are." Students in Alpha actually learned to value each other for the skills and accomplishments shown by their work in the classroom, and often they came to realize something about accepting themselves in the process. One young woman told me how her self-concept was boosted when she realized she understood something an older student did not. She told me this story:

> One day in class meeting, we were discussing the
> computers. There had been several acts of vandalism
> on the computers, and the hard drives were being
> filled with people's work. Someone stated that people
> should not use the "C" drives to save work in; only use
> the "A" drives. This was good advice. Then someone
> asked, 'What's an A drive?' Now, this seemed like an
> innocent question, and it was. What made it stick
> in my mind is the person who asked it. She was an
> ideal student—Alpha's equivalent to a straight A
> student, one who was always willing to communicate,
> collaborate, and use creative and critical thinking. The
> question that she asked was one that was obvious to
> most, and I being the quintessential cyber-chick had
> to resist the urge to scream and jump for joy. Finally
> I had something that I could use to combat!! Finally
> the crack had been discovered in what seemed her
> invulnerable armor? I acquired a feeling of power that
> has not yet dissipated.

Heightened self-awareness and consciousness about ability levels were evident in many of the stories I heard.

The theme approach to curriculum

When I asked Carol Smith about the program's curriculum goals, she told me that as teachers they were always "less concerned with seeing to it that each student had a particular subject or unit than they were with developing a student's ability to seek information, to evaluate it and apply it." Developing curiosity and a disposition to learn were goals teachers had for learners. Teachers involved students in setting curricular objectives and in decisions about activities needed to reach those goals, believing they are motivated to seek new knowledge and skills when they develop an interest in a topic or an idea. Learners are more likely to use information if it has personal meaning, if it fits a frame of reference they understand and especially if it makes a connection to what they know and value. Talking about an interest with others gave students the advantage of multiple perspectives and shared knowledge while also upholding their own contributions to the effort. When Carol was telling me about the process they use to decide on activities that are meaningful for the students, I was reminded of the curricular criteria set by William Smith (cited in Beane, 1997) many years ago:

> *In order to be real, a learning situation must meet certain conditions: (1) It must revolve around problems which are germane to youth; (2) It must be concerned with vital and crucial aspects to the world in which youth is learning to live; and (3) it must call for dynamic and creative behavior on the part of the learner.* (p. 270)

Smith went on to explain that "a sound curriculum would thus consist of a succession of natural and vital units of experience, each centering about a real problem, each drawing upon subject-matter as needed, irrespective of boundary lines, and each eventuating in growth in capacity to live. The development of such a curriculum," Smith pointed out, "obviously calls for more than bringing subjects together into friendly relations under one teacher or, by way of so-called correlation, under several teachers." Beane (1997) extended this thought to the idea that students are the ones who will ultimately integrate the information, not the teachers. The teacher's role then,

Beane suggested, becomes one of guiding students rather than instructing them. This is the role I saw carried out in the Alpha classrooms. Teachers suggested possible topics for study that were relevant and interesting to students and helped students design ways to investigate the topic.

Doubts are often raised about the use of theme studies centering on the question, "Who decides what topic will be studied?" The answer, of course, depends on the intent of the teacher or the purpose of the activity. I saw in more traditionally structured classrooms in Shelburne the theme approach used to study specific content, for example the Westward Movement in American history was used in a social studies class. Guidance counselors in the school used an approach geared toward socio-emotional issues as themes to help students explore aspects of their social and personal world. One such group involved students who had been called together to talk about "getting along with siblings."

Decisions about themes used in Alpha changed over the years of my involvement with the program. What began in the 1970s as teacher-directed activities with input from the students evolved into a process in the late 1980s and early 90s that gave students a major role in the decision. Jim Beane's position about planning curriculum from the "bottom up" was influential in this development. During the early years of the program I saw planning begun with a central theme idea that usually came from teachers or was part of the curricular mandates of the district. Students had a part in deciding and organizing activities around concepts related to themes. One instructional aide, who worked with students on the writing process, told me how she thought exploring a theme contributed to the richness of students' stories. She remembered that one time they were doing a unit about Columbus's voyage, a concept identified in the district's curricular guidelines. She recounted:

> Students had been working on narrative techniques
> while also working on Columbus's journey and reading
> about events of those times. They were working on
> first person narrative and were looking forward to the
> big final culminating project. They were studying the
> science of the era, navigation, astronomy, all kinds of
> things. They had to write a story from the point of view
> of a sailor on one of Columbus's ships. The stories they

produced were magnificent. The way they incorporated
their new knowledge in their stories was wonderful.
They went way out of their way to scour the library to
determine what kinds of birds the sailors would first
hear, and they found out such tidbits as this—the ship
would have not left on a Sunday morning because they
would have gone to Mass first. I thought that was neat.

Actively engaging in the planning of activities associated with a theme unit gave students the opportunity to choose what was meaningful and important for them to learn. It was the beginning of the process of student involvement in their learning that would expand in years ahead as students moved to a more central role in the process.

During the formative years of the late 70s and early 80s, as I came to understand the program, the activities associated with a particular theme usually started with a group of students coming together, sometimes randomly, to investigate a topic they were all interested in. They presented their idea to the teachers, and with them decided on a plan for the study, including a timeline. The exploration and planning sometimes took a week or month to complete while at other times it was finished in hours. One requirement in all group projects remains—after the study was done, students presented their findings to the rest of the class.

> *One requirement in all group projects*
> *remains—after the study was done,*
> *students presented their findings to the*
> *rest of the class.*

Teachers in Alpha told me theme learning provided an effective mediation between two somewhat contrasting young adolescent behaviors. Although students at this age are said to have short attention spans, lack patience with tasks perceived as irrelevant, and have difficulty sorting through large amounts of information, teachers also saw them as curious, enthusiastic, and committed to activities that connected to a broader context. One student told me that when the teachers introduced the topic of "business and the economy" as a general theme, his group developed a popcorn business. He explained to me they were put into groups of five, and when brainstorming his group decided to use advertising to make our popcorn seem better. He said it expressed the opinion that the group's project was "fun" and they "learned a lot."

Project-based learning

Because volunteers were an essential part of the Alpha classroom, community members with a particular expertise in an area (Civil War, electricity, spinning yarn) sometimes came to class to share their knowledge. These presentations often prompted students to investigate a topic further. Students would plan a project outline as a way to organize and represent what they wanted to know. For instance, a geographer came to the class, and his explanation about the formation of the continents brought about an historical study of various countries. After the presentation each of the three teachers decided to study two continents in detail with a group of students. In telling me about this activity one student remembered that he joined the Asia group of just three students. The other students were eighth-grade boys.

> We decided to study the mystery of Anastasia, the Grand Duchess of Russia. In 1918 the Bolsheviks slaughtered the Romans to overthrow the government. There were no remains of Anastasia who was the daughter of the Czar and people thought she may have escaped. The thing I remember the most about this project is our group's final presentation. We made a video of the Romanov murders and interviews after the murders about whether or not Anastasia escaped.

Most students I talk to about project learning remember it as a good way to explore areas that interested them. They had clear memories of the projects they did ranging from single research studies on Koalas to multidimensional units examining systems of the human body or designing and building medieval castles. Besides learning skills of research and inquiry, students told me they valued the opportunity to present their finding in creative ways. Because the culminating events were the high points of the process, students viewed them as representative of their learning. They said they developed a language for talking about learning that friends, especially those in other schools, did not understand. One student told about a time he was talking about his project with a friend who attended a different school. He said he told him his group had just picked out a government project to work on, and he was excited about it. When he asked his friend what project he was working on "he looked at me like I was an alien." He told us he "started to laugh" because he'd "forgotten that other schools don't have themes and projects with culminating events." He was laughing as he was telling this incident years later.

The teacher's role in project learning was first to help students discover topics of interest. In the class after a presentation on the Civil War by a community member, I saw teachers moving from student to student, talking with them, suggesting, questioning, guiding them in the selection of a project related to the theme. Carol Smith noted that one benefit of projects is learning how to learn. During project selection time I listened as teachers asked students questions to help them begin: "What is important to know? How do we find out about these things? What are our resources? How do we access them?" Once students gathered material, teachers then helped them develop a plan for organizing, analyzing, and presenting it.

> *A few times during the year, Alpha students and teachers rolled up their sleeves and dived into an intensive thematic study as a whole class.*

Full-class theme study

A few times during the year, Alpha students and teachers rolled up their sleeves and dived into an intensive thematic study as a whole class. These units often started with a student or small group project and culminated in a presentation to the larger Shelburne community. The first full team study was proposed by two students in 1977. The entire class, students and teachers, began a comprehensive study of the history of Vermont, culminating in a weeklong camping trip to Windsor, the town where Vermont's constitution was signed.

The idea for the study came about when one student was reading about the establishment of Vermont as a state. He interested his friend in the topic, and their discussions prompted the idea of a visit to see the signed document of the state constitution. With teachers' encouragement they decided to propose to the class that all members participate in a study of the "beginnings of Vermont." In preparation for the presentation of their idea to the class, the two boys researched the historical aspects of Windsor and prepared a 12-page typewritten "book" containing significant facts and topics of interest. The book included information about Windsor such as: "The first flag was made there and carried by foot to Hubberton; the electric pump was invented in Windsor; the name Hollywood was created by a man from Windsor." Class members laughed when they heard this seemingly irrelevant information, but their interest was piqued. They wanted to know more about this state in which they lived. The most persuasive information the two boys presented was that Vermont was almost called "New Connecticut." This revelation elicited many hisses from the class.

The class accepted the proposal, and project study began. Everyone in the class had a part in determining what was to be studied and developing the activities and study units that went with the theme. The local paper reported, "Every student did research. There were reports on religion, lodging, industry, justice system, early American banks, and Vermont as an independent country. Each report was presented to the class as background for the culminating trip to the site."

This experience was the beginning of two curricular components of the Alpha program that continue today: integrated theme studies involving the entire class and a weeklong, end-of-the-year camping trip.

This experience was the beginning of two curricular components of the Alpha program that continue today: integrated theme studies involving the entire class and a weeklong, end-of-the-year camping trip. Every year since 1977 come March, students decide on a theme to be studied by the class and a place to hold the year-end camping trip. Full class theme studies in other years included a study of the LaPlatte River Watershed, the Big Alpha Circus, the Middle Ages, and Africa: A Continental Marketplace. Various people connected

32

with Alpha—teachers, parents, students—explained to me in many conversations in several different ways that the concepts and skills aligned with specific disciplines were incorporated in a natural and connected way through the use of themes and projects, especially those associated with the trip. When I asked them why this alliance was important they said they believed that "theme" teaching was compatible with how young adolescents learn. Students always looked forward to the yearly study and the end-of-the-year event.

Is Alpha for everyone?

During this era of expanding numbers and defining curriculum in Alpha, teachers and administrators were often asked by others, and asked themselves if all students were capable of accepting the responsibilities given to students in this classroom. Was Alpha for every student?

Some community members told me "No, youth need direction and structure in order to develop and grow." Such parents did not choose Alpha for their children or did so as a temporary placement for solving specific problems such as to avoid a certain teacher or overcrowding in another classroom. I didn't encounter many of these situations during the years I was associated with Alpha; but there were some, particularly in the early years as the program was evolving and people did not have a clear notion of its philosophy. Students were sometimes caught between the mismatch of parental expectations and program activities. One student told me of his unhappiness with the program. He said:

> The lack of teaching classes is astonishing. If a report is made on a literary piece, it does not receive a grade...there is no History or Science class...Alpha presents too much freedom to the kids. We have a choice: work or don't work. Most any child will choose the don't work option...

Other critics told me they thought the structure of Alpha didn't prepare them for the secondary school. One student told me she had difficulty adjusting to a controlled environment in high school when she left Alpha after five years. She said in the secondary school:

> There were no colorful walls and casual chatter. There were desks and assignments and tests and I felt

*unprepared. After writing articles, conducting research,
and reflecting on my personal experiences, I reached a
conclusion in theory, the program has great potential;
in practice, it does have pitfalls.*

She said she felt her years in Alpha, although happy and
interesting, had not prepared her to adjust to the pressures demanded
at the high school. However, a high school teacher offered a positive
assessment in these words:

*Alpha students seem to ask a little bit more of school
and therefore they ask a little bit more of themselves.
They accept responsibility for their education and give
more to the process.*

The educational theory that gives students the responsibility
for their own learning assumes that given time and encouragement
they will become fully accountable and meet expectations. This
sense of accountability is hard to achieve in one year, especially if
there is conflicting pressure to be somewhere else. There are those
who believe that the individualized nature of the program provides
too much freedom for some students. An instructional aide in Alpha
during the 1980s, who went on to have her own classroom at another
school, puts the issue this way:

*I think, having taught for many years after leaving
Alpha, that probably there are kids for whom it's
not appropriate, but they were okay in a structured
classroom. They just aren't able to handle the openness
of Alpha.*

When I read this statement to administrators and students at
Shelburne, many disagreed. One administrator sees the notion of
self-discipline as a "goal for every student," and the Alpha structure
develops it more than other classrooms. Students are in charge
of their own behaviors, academic and social. The principal of the
elementary school during the years in which the program started
said he had a good deal of faith in the structure of Alpha for teaching
responsibility. He told me he advised parents who had children of
varying learning styles to enroll in Alpha when leaving the primary
level. He said that while the program might be more appealing to
some kids than others, his overall impression was that all kids can
learn in that environment. He conceded the point that some students

adjust quicker than others and that some may need help at the beginning in learning to be more independent; but once given those experiences, they can handle it. Another administrator saw her own concepts about learning change as she saw what was taking place in Alpha. She described this change in these words:

> Over the years I came to watch a cast of characters go through Alpha, and the pleasure of my learning was deepening...I believe that when we talk about the essence of the self-directedness, there is no other way for kids to be in school.

When she compares Alpha kids to those enrolled in a more traditional junior high model she said she didn't know many kids who thrive in the old model. When the social and emotional elements of development are not addressed directly in the curriculum there's still a h-u-g-e portion of themselves that they tuck away and leave at home, and that limits their achievement.

Alpha students were most persuasive. They saw the opportunities provided them to explore and direct their own learning as essential components in their growth as productive and creative beings.

Alpha students were most persuasive. They saw the opportunities provided them to explore and direct their own learning as essential components in their growth as productive and creative beings. One student told me that his parents were concerned that when high school and college came around he would have a hard time. Alpha, his parents suggested to him, may not provide the structure and guidelines he would need to function in a more structured setting. He persuaded his parents to let him remain in Alpha and says as he grew older he realized how helpful the creativity he developed in Alpha was to his growth as a student. As the guidelines got stricter and more rigid as he moved to traditionally structured classes in high school and college, he learned how to find the most original way to stay within them.

By the end of the 1980s, Alpha had evolved into an educational setting where learning depended on self-direction, exploration, working collaboratively, and engaging in a variety of experiences that are usually not found in schools. Did the setting promote responsibility in students, or did responsible students choose this environment? The answer undoubtedly lies somewhere in between and probably depended to a large extent on family beliefs and expectations for the middle school experience. ⚘

The Alpha Team, 1976: Jim Reid, Carol Smith, Susan Wanner, and Warren Stedman. Susan went from being a parent and teaching assistant to becoming an outstanding teacher in her own right with many publications to her credit.

III
Outside Influences

3. To do everything possible to ensure that most of the time the child is happy and free of those outside pressures that really do not need to exist in the belief that she or he will be better.

—Third objective of program, adopted 1971

D uring the late 70s and early 80s Alpha was defining itself, sorting out what was important in the education of its students. Several factors affected the path the program took in its development. Throughout these years questions about who might teach in Alpha, where the program fit in the larger context of the school, and how student learning was to be assessed pushed the administration and the Alpha community to clarify its goals, objectives, and procedures. Sorting through such issues helped the program negotiate its way through somewhat chaotic times to emerge as a viable educational option for families with children in the Shelburne school. Teachers in the program saw these years as ones of "shifting sands" for Alpha.

Several teachers moved in and out of Alpha through the 1980s trying to see if the philosophy fit. All left something of themselves there, a module of study, a song, an assessment technique; but not all found the program comfortable. Determining who would teach in Alpha was a gradual process that continued over 10 years. It involved matching, adapting, and assimilating individual ideas and beliefs into an evolving program philosophy, not an easy task. I observed that teachers and students in Alpha have a very different relationship than exists in other classrooms. The teaching role involved more than the usual concern for student academic performance. I saw teachers doing many things at once, changing gears quickly, answering content questions, and checking on behavioral plans. Their role seemed undefined and somewhat disjointed: they asked questions, suggested references, offered encouragement, admonished students, and put a friendly arm around the shoulder of an upset student. Most conversations were between an individual teacher and an individual student. People who were considering Alpha as a place to teach often spent a day visiting and usually determined rather quickly if this was a fit for them. Some decided "no" after their visit; the activity level and individualized nature of the program was not for them. Others tried it out for a year or two; a very few remained for many years.

Most conversations were between
an individual teacher and an individual student.

When looking for explanations for the match, it seemed to me their placement on the "human contact continuum" was an indicator of their choice. As I listened to teachers describing their decision to stay or not, the level of comfort they felt with teacher-student contact was a factor. Their responses highlighted for me the transition in thinking that had to take place with the education of 10- to 14-year-olds as the move from junior high to middle school occurred. The importance of having teachers for this age group who are willing and able to adapt to student differences in cognitive and social development was recognized.For middle school students it was important to create an environment in which their personal and emotional lives could be acknowledged. Not every teacher, at least in Shelburne at this time, was comfortable with the close student-teacher relationship that Alpha made necessary.

When talking with teachers about the importance of teacher-student relationships I came to understand it as a continuum of interaction. At one end were teachers who saw their main contact with students through the material they presented. They loved the material they were teaching and felt they served students best by passing along content information. They organized their classrooms and class periods around the structure of the discipline they taught. As they prepared their lessons they worried most about the material students needed to learn to move on to a more specialized study. For them love of subject was how they displayed love of student.

Further along the continuum came those who understood that dealing with the content alone missed many crucial aspects of an education. Some teachers believe learning must be practical and have relevance in the lives of their students. Planning activities that connect them to the world outside the classroom was their focus; their main goal was to make learning germane. Their contact with students was through the activities they planned.

Beyond them stand teachers who believed that teaching involved making connections with each student on many levels, intellectual, personal, social. They defined successful teaching as "getting to know the hopes, fears, and potential of each student." They did not follow a standard approach to learning or teaching; they individualized expectations and activities for students. They were as concerned about student identity development and self-understanding as they were about the content presented and activities planned. These are the teachers who belong in Alpha. A graduate of Alpha expressed the special student-teacher relationship in these words:

> *My teachers and I have a strong bond. She became a friend, someone I could go to, someone I could trust with any of my problems. Once you get to know an adult that way, and admire and respect them that way, you are much more likely to listen to what they have to say.*

Although many teachers were intrigued by the idea of teaching in an alternative setting, a small number chose it for a career. A few—Linda Mann, Than James, Meg Kenny—believed in the philosophy, stayed with the program a few years while they learned to implement it, and moved to other educational settings where they carried the Alpha vision with them. Those who stayed with the program for years, Jim Reid, the creator, Warren Steadman who stayed for 15 years, and Carol Smith for 25, believed the most important aspect of teaching was to establish trusting relationships with students, giving them the freedom to explore, experiment, and test limits, along with the opportunity and skills to connect to others. What set them apart from other teachers was their belief in children's ability to guide their own leaning. When reflecting on the characteristics he had envisioned for teachers in the program Jim, the founding teacher, said:

> I think teaching has to be less teacher centered and more child centered…You have to have a high tolerance for ambiguity and political structure…You have to be willing to not know the answer, not be sure you've accomplished everything, not to think you know a child's potential…you have to know when to stay out of the way and when to move ahead…

This view of teaching asked those fulfilling the role to possess substantial knowledge about the nature and development of students and a good deal of self-assurance about their own actions. I observed that the connections teachers made with students were often a result of their personal style. Alpha teachers had positive self-identities. They sought advice from others and each other routinely, and they indicated to me they were learning "a good deal from students in their daily interactions."

The program was organized so that individual teachers each had responsibility for a small group of students, pulling them together at least weekly in what was termed their "prime time group." These groups provided one means of helping teachers get to know students. During prime time meetings teachers assisted students in identifying areas of interest. They encouraged students with common interests to work together in groups or pairs pointing out that investigations are often richer and more meaningful when they are shared with others. When I asked teachers in Alpha about the importance of teaching

Students with common interests work together in groups on projects.

content they said they thought the other aspects of a student's development were as important as academic performance per se; therefore, they emphasized content in relation to student needs. For example, they told me they "teach social studies so students learn how to become good citizens" by showing them how "to live and act responsibly," and they teach math so students can learn "how to make change and pay taxes;" "reading, writing, spelling so students can communicate effectively with others." The most important thing they feel they do is to entrust students with important choices concerning their own education, including "How can I learn this?" "What should I study?" "How can I structure responses?" and when to move on. Teachers who made a commitment to the program were as concerned with the development of positive self-understanding and identity for students as they were with specific factual content or method of presentation. Although they encouraged students to study mathematics if their interest suggested such a study, they understood that they should not "create an environment in the classroom where mathematical competence defined a student's self-worth."

The most remembered characteristic of Alpha teachers identified by former students was the way their teachers believed in their potential and abilities, seeing them as responsible for their words and actions and attributing the best of motives to their responses. One alumnus told me:

> Our teachers had so much faith in us that they allowed
> us to make decisions about our class, make our own
> goals, plan our own time; and all of this was done with
> just a few words of wisdom and guidance from them.

41

Two structural aspects of the program's organization supported strong teacher-student relationships—the team teaching approach to instruction and the multiyear grouping. With more than one teacher in the room, students had options about who to connect with, confide in. There was opportunity to back away from one teacher and connect with another. One student told me about a teacher she didn't work with very often because of his "out of the ordinary ways of acting." When describing him she said, "let's just say he was very different with his teaching methods. He didn't come across with the same caring nature as other teachers." When I asked her what she meant, she told me he used other methods for teaching, including yelling. Since this behavior didn't seem in line with what I saw or had heard about Alpha teachers from other students, I asked her if that had affected her learning and desire to be in the program. She told me that she "personally didn't have any problems with him, but he had problems with other students." As grave as her allegations sound, and contrary to characteristics desired for teachers in the program, the important point to her story, I thought, was that she was able to work with another teacher because of the team approach. She told me she could bypass him and still keep on with her learning. In a single-teacher classroom, her learning would have been slowed, and she would have had to change class or sit silently through the year.

Because of the multiyear aspect of Alpha, teachers' roles evolved and changed during the years. One parent described the change in role by telling me teachers "went from being a mother figure to the fourth graders to being a mentor figure by the time they were in eighth grade." Five years gave students and teachers time to have many experiences together, learn many sides of each other, and work through interpersonal conflicts and tense moments. Students told me they learned that teachers, like friends, are not without faults, make mistakes, and admit errors. When responding to inquiries about teacher-student interactions, one student told this story:

> We were doing a unit on life. There were three different
> groups, and I was in the Community Group. For my
> final project, I was doing a booklet for children about
> the history of Shelburne, because the history books in
> the library were verbose and confusing. I handed it
> in on the Friday before winter break, ready to return

*to school so I could show it off at the exhibit that was
going to occur. On the night of the exposition, I looked
everywhere for my project. It was nowhere to be found.
Puzzled and upset, I sought out the teacher. She gave
me a pitying look and draped her arm around me. She
said, "I have bad news." She turned red. "My cats peed
on your project." Horrified, I watched as she showed
me the remnants of my booklet. It was stained yellow,
wrinkled, and smelled awful.*

As disturbing as this was for the student at the time, it was
one encounter of many with this teacher over the years. Time
allowed them to negotiate their relationship through this difficult
situation. She told me that in the end that particular experience
actually strengthened their relationship. It gave her insight into the
"humanness" of teachers; and because they were together each day
over the next three years, such tense moments could be worked
through. As I listened to this story, I thought how fortunate she was
to have had time to get beyond an experience that might have ended
a connection.

Student-teacher relationships established in Alpha remain
strong through the years. When asked years later about their
relationships with teachers, past students variously talked about them
as their "friends," "parents," and "role models." They told me they
remembered "calling them by first names," and some said that the
interactions with teachers in Alpha "helped them establish wonderful
relationships with high school and college teachers by showing them
how to accept others, resolve differences, and remain connected."

A very few connections have turned into lasting professional
relationships, as when a former student became a teacher. The
mother of an alumnus attributed her daughter's choice of vocation to
the Alpha program and the close connections made with its teachers.
"She wants to teach because of that program. I mean she really feels
she can make a difference for kids just as her teachers did for her."
The several alumni I interviewed who became teachers told me they
developed a new special relationship with their former teachers. As
I heard them talk about the influence Alpha teachers had on them I
thought that although light years away from each other in experience
and age, they became contemporaries in the realm of professional
education. Ten, 20 years later the teacher and former student
communicate as equals in the sphere of teaching—a new kind of

delight for both. One who had been teaching for eight years told me about the influence of Carol Smith on her teaching. She said:

> As I was talking with Carol about my class, I realized that I wouldn't be the teacher I am today if I had not been in Alpha. It taught me that learning is connected, and just understanding one side isn't enough. Discussing my profession with Carol now, I feel smart and self-confident. Looking around my classroom, I see Alpha. Seats in circles, students' work hanging from every nook and cranny. I remember how much my teachers in Alpha cared for me and I try to do the same for each of my students. My relationship with Carol, changing from teacher to friend to colleague, has taught me how to be connected and that I might change the world in my own little way.

Teachers make the difference between successful learning experiences and non-successful ones. Through the 1980s, deciding who should teach in the Alpha Program created some problems both within the program and outside the classroom. Deciding on the characteristics that would best exemplify the mission of the program was not an easy task. Defining a profile of teacher traits that match the complexities of the program, especially as it was evolving, was difficult. There was input from everyone—administrators, parents, and students—when making staffing decisions; and both potential teachers and the program tried to adjust to various preferences. In the end those who ended up staying were committed to the philosophy that had become Alpha; they were full of enthusiasm, warmth, and a genuine belief in the power of connections. They also had an ability to plan and a vast knowledge of individual difference and personal development. Administrators may have asked certain candidates to consider Alpha as a teaching position, but program philosophy and structure selected those who came to be trusted and respected as Alpha members. Teachers who were most successful in Alpha were secure in their own identities and possessed educational values that clearly matched the basic tenets of the program. Stories that students told me revealed that their teachers were very influential in helping them figure out their lives as adolescents and future adults.

Finding a niche within the school

The solidifying years of the 1980s were difficult ones for the teachers who stayed in the Alpha program. They often felt ostracized, cut off from colleagues with limited resources to draw on for program and personal support. They were reminded by the administration that resources were divided among all classrooms which meant no extra resources for starting something new, no additional time allotted for planning, no incentives monetary or other benefits for working in the program. The teachers felt scrutinized by other teachers in the building, by community members who questioned the assumed cost of providing an alternative program, and by the administration who supported their efforts with words but little else. The teachers told me they knew working together as a team was essential for their own peace of mind and for the success of the students. They needed to share information about student performance and progress since they all interacted with every student sometime during the day. They also knew that they needed each other for support.

With no common planning time to discuss various elements of the program, teachers met whenever they could—usually after school and sometimes long into the evening. The instructional aide during the early years told me these conversations moved from specific instances to general concerns:

> Almost every afternoon, we would talk for a while. It was always the same pattern…We would look at the problem that had arisen or the successes we had. Talk about what we were doing and then it would move to the metacognitive level. We'd talk about why we were doing it. How did this fit into the whole vision of what we were trying to achieve here. So everyday talk was at the philosophical level.

These discussions were important for the development of the curricular aspects of Alpha because they put the "everydayness" of activities into a broader context. The teachers told me during this time they were "reminded of why they were there." These meetings also provided personal support for them as pressures to justify and validate this way of learning intensified. School board members began asking about the cost; parents questioned student performance; colleagues wondered about the curriculum provided and whether Alpha students would be prepared for high school.

Other teachers and classrooms in the middle school began to feel some backlash from the alternative nature of the curriculum offered in Alpha. Those opposed to teaching anything but basic skills and content objected to suggestions for even minor innovations in their classrooms. The principal listened to parental concerns and told me that any time another teacher wanted to introduce a new kind of program or something that was different from a conventional program, parents would say to other teachers, "if we'd wanted Alpha, we would have chosen it." Not only had the alternative nature of the curricular structure in Alpha designated it to a category of "different," other classrooms became identified as "regular" and were limited to "known" curricular options. To some in the community Alpha became the rival. It was more than an alternative curricular option; it symbolized what some did not want identified with education in Shelburne. The principal of the primary school commented that when talking to parents about their choices for placement in the middle grades "the minute people heard that kids aren't taught in a lock-step method, they assumed it's Alpha." Some teachers welcomed this distinction because it confirmed the way they had been teaching for years. Others, ready to try new pedagogical ideas, feared parental pressure and hesitated to try new activities or approaches to learning.

> *The debate on assessment of student learning and performance accountability measures brought the Alpha program under closer scrutiny by other teachers and people in the community.*

The dynamics inside the school polarized as the Alpha philosophy crystallized distinctly different from the other classrooms. Family decisions about placement for children were influenced by curricular options, a positive twist from an educational theorist's standpoint but not seen as such from some parent and practitioner views. Alpha stood in contrast to the education provided by the rest of the school, both in philosophy and organizational structure. As they saw it, the choices were limited, Alpha or Regular. At school board meetings community members questioned the equal distribution of resources to classrooms, reasoning that a program so different from others surely must cost more. Regular teachers shied away from activities that might be associated with individualized learning or "Alpha-like" structure. Alpha teachers worked hard to keep the classroom free of outside pressures that could influence the structure and organization they had built, but the job was not an easy one. The development of the Alpha "alternative" in Shelburne created waves throughout the community and school that remained for years.

Assessment tension

During the winter months of 1978, Jim, the founding teacher of Alpha, challenged new forms of student assessment mandated by the state and the district. The conflict that ensued led to Jim's dismissal. The state had determined that each school in Vermont must measure yearly student performance on tests of basic competencies. The district not only concurred with this mandate but added a checklist of its own. Jim's reason for the challenge was that the evaluation forms and checklist did not measure adequately or substantially what students were learning in Alpha or what the philosophy of the program deemed important. His argument fundamentally was a philosophical one. The assessment process, adopted by the State Board of Education for every school in every district in the State of Vermont, countered every learning goal set for the alternatively designed program. The "cards" adopted by the Chittenden South Supervisory District (CSSD) of which Shelburne was a part, duplicated, in his mind, the errors of the state assessment program. Although most teachers in the Shelburne system did not have the philosophical objection that Jim had, they did feel that there was "too much paperwork" to make the system manageable and in the beginning supported Jim in his challenge.

Jim criticized both systems, state and district, as "dictating a detailed sequence of learning." Other teachers in Shelburne eventually agreed to support the use of the system mandated by the state, but they wanted to do so on alternate years cutting down the amount of paperwork required. They also refused to use the district "cards." The local newspaper quoted one teacher who summarized the objections saying the detail of the district cards "requires excessive testing and record keeping which takes away from actual teaching time and does not realistically evaluate the student's progress." Teachers argued they were filling out forms for the district that were actually duplicate evaluations with the state forms. They moved the argument from one that was philosophical to a more practical one. After much persuasion by his colleagues, Jim agreed to maintain one set of records, the state's list of student competencies. The Shelburne school board, supported by the district board, demanded two, and after lengthy debate and several public hearings, the board voted to dismiss Jim, effective March 15, 1978.

The superintendent, Theodore Whalen, admitted that he didn't like to "lose a good teacher," but "here the individual is not as important as the system." In a letter from the school board chair, Jim's dismissal was justified because he refused to carry out a reasonable order of the superintendent—"insubordination" was the reason given. The discussion on assessment had moved yet again, from a practical issue to a personnel matter. In his statement

Jim Reid in a 1981 photograph.

before the Shelburne Board of Directors, Jim denied that he had failed to carry out a reasonable order, arguing that any order which "requires me to shortchange children in the name of educational progress cannot be reasonable." While many Shelburne teachers supported Jim's position and spoke publicly in his defense, none were willing or able to stand with him in the final protest. They valued their teaching positions in Shelburne and were not willing to jeopardize their jobs for the principle involved. Jim left in the middle of the school year. He remained in Vermont for another year, then became principal of a progressive school in Philadelphia founded on the principles of John Dewey. The conflict over assessment influenced the Alpha program and was not resolved for years.

The debate on assessment of student learning and performance accountability measures brought the Alpha program under closer scrutiny by other teachers and people in the community. The teachers left in Alpha, Carol and Warren, were in the difficult position of figuring out a way to incorporate outside demands for performance measurements into a program that was philosophically opposed to such external assessment. They reluctantly used the CSSD "cards" and the state competency checklists during the late 1970s to comply with administrative mandates but tried not to let student results on these measures influence classroom activities. They reported scores when they were told to do so but did little else with the information.

One thing this controversy did do was to focus the attention of Alpha members on the area of assessment and evaluation. Throughout the rest of that year and into the next, students, parents, and teachers in Alpha debated, designed, and tried out several means of demonstrating what students know and were able to do within the framework of a student-centered program. The goal was to provide something better than the existing checklists, one that would demonstrate performance levels appropriate for the curricular goals of Alpha. They had learned that the goals and their measurement must be understandable to those not involved in the program; they must align with state and district mandates, and they must clearly articulate what it was students had learned. Pressures outside the classroom, particularly those having to do with evaluation and assessment, were shaping activities in Alpha, and how members coped with these pressures influenced future directions and definition of the program.

A new way of measuring

A study group of Alpha members led by the teachers looked at the area of student assessment during the next two years and came up with a system that still is intact today. In their search for the "right" system, members found many interesting paradoxes related to assessment. They found standardized measurements to be the most commonly known means of evaluating learning because they are an efficient and easy means of measuring performance. They described standardized measurements as those that asked students to respond to questions devised by experts about specific content. These instruments are normed to national grade level standards so parents can see where their children rank in comparison to others. The results are also compared by grade level across the country with no regard for context, type of district, location of school, classroom organization, curriculum structure, or the availability of resources.

During the 1980s all students in the Shelburne schools were tested using standardized measurements every other year. Students in Alpha demonstrated mixed performance results on these tests. When testing material that students had included as part of their individual plans, they did well. If the tests asked for content knowledge commonly covered for a particular grade level but not part of an individual student's plan, they did poorly. If they had studied the content, they could answer the questions; if they hadn't, they couldn't. The fear expressed by Jim during the testing controversy became obvious in this context—scores on standardized measurements were not indicative of what students in Alpha had studied or were able to do. A mismatch existed between what students knew and what was deemed important by the questions on the tests. Because the pressure from the district office and the local school board to administer standardized measurements was great, Alpha teachers found themselves constantly in the position of explaining students' scores to parents and administrators and debating among themselves the refinement of curricular activities to match what was to be measured, a practice they felt worked against student-directed curricular choices.

> *...scores on standardized measurements were not indicative of what students in Alpha had studied or were able to do.*

Alpha teachers and parents often were asked throughout these years at public meetings how they managed assessment of student learning when goals were individualized and not grade level dependent. How would they be able to tell if students made sufficient progress without some standardized measurements? The teachers felt the most adequate response was an explanation of the program philosophy and a description of how they relied on individualized work to show progress toward goals that had been set by the students themselves. They told me they used information about what had been learned in project reports, portfolios of edited work, teacher observations, and conferences with students to determine progress toward goals. Intended outcomes were individualized. Several times during the year, I observed teacher-student conferences where students talked about their learning and teachers questioned them about their progress. Records were kept of these meetings documenting progress toward goals. Teachers told me this was a time-intensive system of assessment but seemed much more authentic than more traditional pencil and paper tests of achievement.

One outcome of the "CSSD cards controversy" was that teachers and parent leaders in Alpha realized the importance of communicating program standards and performance criteria to those not directly involved in the classroom. They learned something about public relations. Because they held onto the notion that no letter grades (A, B, C...) would be given, clear explanations about student progress were essential. Alpha leaders began to design a process that made sense for this program. It detailed general goals and expectations that could be applied across grade levels and content areas.

The teachers began the process of defining an assessment procedure by listing criteria that became part of the evaluation protocol and gave students a guide for completing work. For example, in the area of writing it was expected that each student would

- Have a writing in progress at all times
- Number and date all drafts of a piece of writing
- Conference with another student and with a teacher at least once before finalizing a piece of writing
- Keep finished writings (with all drafts attached) in his or her working portfolio to be reviewed
- Keep an ongoing list of misspelled words
- Identify ten new spelling and vocabulary words.

The belief about learning that underlies this part of assessment, teachers told me, was that the points outlined "habits" of good learners that promoted successful performance and encouraged high levels of academic achievement. Students recorded progress in each of the stated areas in their assessment notebooks. The guide gave students an outline of what must be done in order to complete successfully an assignment, and it offered them a means of improving their writing. The notebook was a tool for teachers to use in monitoring student progress. Check-ins with teachers during weekly conferences gave students information about areas in their writing that still needed work and gave teachers information about skill areas, spelling, punctuation, or content deficits that needed to be addressed. Workshops in specific areas were held for students needing assistance.

Progress toward goals was measured individually for each student. Student activity reports were compared to previous records of accomplishment in order to indicate gains. Using a rubric checked by teachers with such indicators as *not yet, almost, you're there!* students left the weekly conference knowing how and in what areas their writing needed improvement. The student decided when a piece of work was to be submitted to the teacher as a final product. At that time it was added to a writing portfolio and submitted for a summative assessment using stated criteria:

- Student writes with purpose
- Writing is organized
- Student uses details that are appropriate to purpose and that support the main idea
- Student writing reflects personal voice and expression
- Student writing exhibits correct grammar, usage, and mechanics.

Similar expectations and progress criteria were established for math, social studies, and science. This process involved students in planning and assessing their own activities. It encouraged them to be accountable, taking responsibility for their own learning and asking them to document and explain what they know and were able to do.

Students often shared their progress with others, sometimes at public meetings. One way they did this was by creating learning summaries of their work that they presented to classmates, parents, and community members during an evening event called Learning Night. Community and family members were invited to hear students talk; guests were invited to ask questions about what they heard. People who had attended these events told me they were impressed with the work that was done and the way students described what they knew. The guidance counselor of the school remarked, "You don't have the A B C grade and you don't have a math score...but you just listen to those kids describing and explaining what they've done. I'm just blown away every Learning Night."

Comparative achievement data placed Alpha students well ahead of their age and grade level peers.

From the time of the assessment controversy, Alpha students participated in school-wide standardized testing where their scores were compared across schools and grade levels. During the late 1980s Shelburne schools adopted the Scholastic Achievement Test for students in grades five and seven and the New Standard Reference exams in reading, writing, and math. Since these generalized areas of study were emphasized in all projects for Alpha students they performed as well or better than the rest of the school in those areas and significantly better than comparable students in the district and the state. Comparative data placed Alpha students well ahead of their age and grade level peers. Had the mandate for district and statewide testing forced the tailoring of curriculum activities in Alpha to conform to measurement guidelines? When asked about this Carol Smith told me

> With all the worry of integrated curriculum not giving students enough exposure to the disciplines, it seems our students do well. It is not the content of the disciplines that improves scores but the DOING of the discipline—being a scientist, a historian, a writer, or a mathematician—that makes the difference. Our students have those opportunities throughout their three years on our team.

The new way of demonstrating what students in Alpha know became so acceptable to parents that emphasis on standardized scores was minimized once this system was in place; parents were less concerned about low scores in specific areas; administrators were more tolerant of mixed test results; teachers had less need for lengthy explanations; and students were less anxious about taking the tests.

Although outside influences inevitably crept into the learning environment, class members used these as opportunities to refine Alpha. Had the assessment issue not erupted, had the program been left to evolve assessment measurements on its own, would these tensions have surfaced? To some degree the answers are unimportant. Teachers and parents of students from this era told me the impressive thing about this time was the way people responded to this threat to program philosophy. One parent noted, "They just picked up the challenge and made something of it."

Members of Alpha had designed a means of assessment that was compatible with its program goals and philosophy, a major achievement. Perhaps one student's response to my questions about documentation of learning explains best the progress that had been made following Jim's resignation:

> Today I sat down to watch the tape of my eighth grade Alpha video projects. I remember being seated around a table in Carol's Prime Time when the teachers explained to us the concepts of learning summaries. We would have to respond to 12 or 14 questions regarding our progress as effective learners. The questions required answers backed by specific examples of times when we had demonstrated progress in an area of learning. We discussed how we would turn in our responses, and students began to ask questions. But as this was happening my mind began to work on how I could most effectively express my development as a learner. I asked a question that I already knew the answer to: "Does it have to be written?" I don't think they quite knew what to expect, but the last thing they would have done was say "yes." So I sat in a corner and wrote the script to a short movie that contained all my answers, the way I could best express them.

A bit about standards

During the late 1980s and early 1990s learning standards were developed at both the state and national levels that outlined what students were expected to know and be able to do. Designed to give teachers (and students) a clear picture of what was expected and a timeline within which to work, the standards themselves were not meant as a delivery method, but rather an end result.

When the State of Vermont crafted its standards, called the *Common Core of Learning*, Alpha began to purposefully integrate the ideas put forth in that document. The *Common Core of Learning* consisted of descriptions of the skills desired for each student called the *Vital Results*. The standards were in the areas of *Communication, Reasoning and Problem Solving, Personal Development*, and *Civic and Social Responsibility*. In addition, *Fields of Knowledge* standards were identified that addressed discipline-specific areas of knowledge. Students used standards from both of these documents to organize their work for the week. For each theme studied or project designed, students identified the most important standards to be addressed. Each report or project involved the use of 3-6 specific standards that were purposefully assessed at the end of the study. Although many standards could be identified for each activity, it was important to enumerate the ones that would be addressed consciously.

Some have argued that the standards movement derails learning, fragmenting the outcome and causing students to focus on specific knowledge and skills. When I talked to Alpha teachers about this point they disagreed saying that the movement "has not been problematic for Alpha or its students." They told me that they felt the Vermont standards, organized in clusters of *Vital Results, Fields of Knowledge,* and *Learning Opportunities,* as well as in multiyear spans have given them permission to continue the work they believe in. They say that much of what the *Common Core of Learning* proposes is "what we have been doing" and see as best practice for work in the middle grades. They gave this example of how the standards were addressed in an environmental theme focusing on three different habitats.

> *Defining the characteristics and purpose of each habitat (knowledge) gave students the foundation on which to build their investigation into what lives in each habitat, how habitats are different and the same, and how habitats are connected. This study offered many opportunities to develop specific skills in science: use of the microscope, plant and animal identification, soil and water testing (all standards in the science field of knowledge) as well as skills that fall in the Vital Results standards such as ability to sort, classify, observe, compare/contrast, and analyze. The field work itself allowed students to use these skills as they investigated the habitat under study. Field journals offered ways to record the investigations, again doing the work of real scientists and naturalists.*

Teachers told me there was a dual purpose here: "to understand the classification system for plants and animals, and to use that system in an authentic way." They argued that assessment practices must create opportunities for students to connect and make sense of the pieces of their learning; students must be given opportunities to use their skills and knowledge to demonstrate their understanding of issues and ideas. This is what the newly designed assessment process in Alpha was to do. Involving students in the discussion of the standards to be addressed with each learning activity gave them a clear picture of what they should know and be able to do. The *Vermont Common Core of Learning* as represented through the *Vital Results* and *Fields of Knowledge* provided a framework to address topics and design appropriate and relevant assessment measures.

By the end of the 1980s Alpha members had faced many pressures from within and outside the classroom. They were in many senses "weather-beaten," as one teacher phrased it, by these experiences. However, these conflicts served some useful purposes. Working through the tensions helped members of the program clarify their philosophy further, refining it to meet the context and demands of the time. They now had a better understanding of the kind of teacher who would be comfortable carrying out the program's philosophy. The Alpha program had achieved a definite place in the school and a solid identity, even as an alternative, in the educational realm of the village of Shelburne. And, to boot, a workable and authentic assessment system had been designed. With a multiage student-centered program they were now ready to look inward and further strengthen the learning community that had been forged. ⭐

*Alpha teachers were not just observers
of activities but participants.
Can you find the teachers?*

IV
Internalizing

4. To lead the child to a form of self-discipline that will carry over to those situations where it will be the only discipline worth having.

—Fourth objective of program, adopted 1971

Following the years of formation and definition for the Alpha program, members began to examine more intensely the learning that was happening in the program. Students were encouraged to look at themselves and learn who they were as individuals by studying the complex and varied changes taking place in their bodies and their social world. They also discovered the importance of working together. These were the aspects of Alpha that made it a genuine learning community and kept it strong over the years.

Self-understanding

Because the curriculum in Alpha was designed around student interests and needs, teachers helped students investigate and understand themselves, appreciating different aspects of their developing selves. The individualized nature of the curriculum encouraged the exploration of differing aspects of the self along with self-assessments that helped students understand their desires and needs. Students learned to value and accept themselves. The lives of young adolescents, especially today, are at risk if their surroundings do not meet their social and emotional needs. Alpha teachers believed what was needed in school was a rich environment where developmentally appropriate curriculum included adolescent health and well being issues. They knew the experiences students have in the middle grades affect their sense of identity and orientation to the world for years to come. I often heard teachers discuss with students developmental growth in general and specific student behaviors. The lessons in Alpha often were about the world of adolescence, examining those aspects of behavior they could control. Students learned about transitions that take place physically, socially, and emotionally within their own bodies and minds as a way of understanding their actions within the classroom and beyond. I regularly saw students displaying different levels of development.

Working in groups helps students learn more about themselves.

At one point, I saw a student sitting alone stacking blocks one on top of another; an hour later that same student was working on a complicated project with other students, dismantling, repairing, and reassembling an automobile. The flexibility of the classroom environment helped students match needs with activities that met those wants. The rich, multifaceted landscape of adolescent life was evident here. The smiling faces of students who told me stories often betrayed what was happening in their lives. As an observer in the program I heard stores that ranged from silly jokes shared with a friend to ones of an unbearable inner pressure toward the taking of their lives. In her work on adolescent development, author Mary Pipher (1994) terms this the "search for solid ground" as students adjust to numerous changing demands. What I saw were many youngsters looking for sturdy footing as they negotiated their lives with peers, teachers, and parents. The multiage, individually directed focus present in Alpha gave students opportunity and encouragement to identify their emotions and desires as they met the challenges of early adolescence. An eighth grader expressed appreciation for assistance in growing up with these words:

> You have given me the time and space to explore myself, my learning, and my growth. You must be part of a special breed of teachers who were not afraid of taking chances, not afraid to try new things, not afraid of criticism, not afraid of anything. Thank you for giving me the time for learning and discovery and growth.

Working in groups helped students learn more about themselves. In Alpha the social world of school was organized with peers of varying grade and age levels. Students worked together, sharing tasks and information about projects and confiding personal thoughts with each other as well. They took time to listen to each other and learned to act as a group in supporting one another. Beliefs about what is important in education were apparent in the organization of space and activities in Alpha. I noticed that as students worked in this program these beliefs gradually became their own. My talks with students and teachers as well as with parents and paraprofessionals in the classroom made it evident that Alpha members learned a good many skills besides how to add, subtract, multiply, and divide—such as how to work with others, how to love, how to take criticism, and how to experience joy. Although students in Alpha were certainly caught in the confusion of pubertal changes, full of doubts, fears, and anxieties about themselves and the world around them, they found a comfortable place in Alpha in which to examine the transformations taking place. Alumni's stories suggested that by the time students were ready to leave the program they had learned to value their own uniqueness and the importance of connecting with others.

...what adolescents need most is "access to a range of legitimate opportunities" and "long-term support from adults who deeply care about them."

Teachers learned from students that what adolescents need most is "access to a range of legitimate opportunities" and "long-term support from adults who deeply care about them." The climate established in the formative years of the program, as I came to understand it, encouraged class members to learn about themselves by developing a capacity to care about others.

Defining community

The Alpha classroom was set apart from the rest of the school physically, philosophically, and by the activities planned in the curriculum. While students worked independently and in small groups through most of the day, they came together regularly to participate in activities as a whole class. This provided all members of Alpha time to practice the basics of a democratic community, fundamentals that tie the rights of individuals with principles of living with others. Part of learning about themselves involved dis-covering ways to express their own needs and desires within a group.

Shared experiences became part of the weekly classroom routine. Every Friday morning students gathered in the community space for "Read Aloud," a time when the class shared the reading of a story. Students remember this time fondly and told me about it in their stories. One recalled how reading a particular story made a "lasting impression" on her in fourth grade. She was sitting on the newly constructed loft in the room among all her classmates when

> Carol was reading **Where the Red Fern Grows.** When
> she came towards the end she was crying too much to
> continue, so she passed the book off to an eighth grade
> girl. Tracy read on for awhile before she had to pass the
> book on and so forth for several readers.

She said years later it is "still one of my favorite books." As I observed her expression as she talked, the lasting impact this experience had on her was evident. The important thing about this activity, it seems, is that it not only fostered love of literature but reading aloud to the whole group connected them to each other through shared emotion.

The teachers in Alpha believed that while shared experiences were important, they were not enough to promote community values. They claimed, "Community is built by arranging activities intended to contribute to its growth." There is an intentional part to creating community. The focus of many of the activities in Alpha was to promote interaction between class members giving them opportunities to relate to each other in various situations. Teachers said they hoped these experiences would build a collective set of understandings, a shared history, which would become the basis of an active community. One student thought the yearly "sleepover" was such an event. She said that during the early years of the program all class members came to school after dinner prepared to spend the night together. She described the scene as "sleeping bags spread across the AV room floor to watch a movie that had been voted on by the class." She remembered, "people gathered around the piano in their pajamas enjoying a sing-along." She said these nights were filled with "laughing, sharing stories, and talking far into the night." Through relaxed conversations and exchanges that were part of evenings such as this, students came to know each other in a different way. Another student told me the benefit of the sleepover was that when the "next morning after we made breakfast and headed back to class to start another day of school, I often took with me a new friend, a common joke, a collective experience." As Alpha grew in size the sleepover was discontinued, much to the surprise of alumni who exclaimed when I told them, "What, no sleepover!!!"

Several events were planned throughout the years to increase the community feeling. One was the "pig out," a whole class dinner involving students, teachers, and family members. Events such as this helped students broaden their perspectives about each other, getting to know each other in a personal context, and perhaps increasing their tolerance for understanding different ways of being.

Many educators believe that a central mission of schooling is the development of civic character and the critical reasoning skills needed to promote and sustain democratic governance. Schools, then, need to be not only examples of democratic principles, but ones who graduate young people who will want to live a democratic way of life. This thinking was influential to the development of Alpha. Jim Reid talked to me about his belief in the importance of providing a classroom where democratic values were practiced. He, and the teachers who joined him as Alpha developed genuinely believed that the quality of life in a democratic society is directly related to effective decision making on the part of its citizens, and they wanted to establish a classroom where the development of these skills was possible. Teachers' comments indicated they knew working in this way would require effort and a good deal of compromise for all but was important enough to set aside time each week to discuss community issues.

Weekly class meeting time was set aside to discuss student issues and concerns.

Class meeting

In Alpha, weekly class meeting time was set aside to discuss student issues and concerns. It took on several organizational structures through the years and continues as a part of the program. Once a week the entire class came together to talk about issues and problems shared by class members. Familiar with the town meeting concept still popular as a means of citizen participation in Vermont towns and villages, students liked the idea that they had an opportunity to govern themselves. They voted on officers during the first meeting; a class moderator, secretary, and treasurer were chosen. These might change from year to year. One student told about his experience as moderator of the class meeting when the rules changed.

> *I had always been semi-conscious of the dynamics of our group discussion and relationships as a community, but this never struck me so much as the year that our class meetings changed from being run by Robert's Rules of Order to consensus. It was at this first meeting that we would choose the theme for the trip, which even by democracy was a heated*

and lengthy discussion. That afternoon held one long and frustrating meeting—but with a few gut-wrenching compromises, we made it successfully through. And at the end of it all, besides learning how to keep my patience and moderate without inflicting my own prejudices, I began developing a sensitivity to everyone's perspectives and became proficient at devising ways to accommodate everyone.

When students talked about the benefits of class meetings, they often mentioned the many skills they gained that helped them learn how to actively participate in community discussions. They learned "how to listen closely," "articulate positions," "reason logically," and "persuade their peers." Preparing to present an issue at class meetings helped them learn how to organize their thoughts. Once students presented the issue, the class usually divided into committees to investigate different aspects of it during the week. At the next class meeting committees presented what they had found out, and a full class discussion ensued. Perhaps the most important idea that students learned through this process was that decision making sometimes involves conflicting interests and desires. In discussions at these meetings, students formed opinions, changed their minds, and negotiated viewpoints to present new suggestions. Sometimes they gave up personal choice for the good of the group; other times they persuaded the group to accept their preference. These discussions and interactions demonstrated how those with opposing views can work toward a common goal.

Many stories told by students were about the discussion of ideas or events that took place during class meeting time. Several recalled with satisfaction and a bit of delight the result of their attempt to convince classmates of a particular point of view. One student related the following story:

Every year Alpha makes a quilt...Everyone in the whole Alpha team has to agree on one design and color scheme. I was in the midst of 70 or so fellow-Alpha students during class meeting to decide on the pattern for the quilt. The quilt was a big deal to us because it was what we would be manufacturing for the next two months or so, then raffling off. Hard work goes into it; it is not easy to partially design, sew, and

*then go door-to-door to sell tickets for the raffle of this
quilt. For some reason I and two of my friends really
wanted this one pattern. The whole rest of the class
wanted a different pattern. When that group asked
for consensus, the three of us objected. After hours of
convincing the rest of the class that our pattern was the
best, the three of us succeeding in convincing them that
our pattern should be used.*

He went to tell me about the lessons he learned from this experience,
those of "perseverance" and "persuasiveness." He ended this
story by explaining how class meetings taught him about the
possibilities inherent in using a process that gives everyone a chance
to participate and, in this case, "the minority had overcome the
majority." An instructional aide in Alpha said she thought class
meeting was a "magnificent process where kids learned how to
interact and look through all issues involved with a wait before
deciding; hear each other out, and weigh the consequences."
Students saw the value of a participatory democracy by practicing it.

*"Hard work goes into it; it is not easy to partially design, sew, and
then go door-to-door to sell tickets for the raffle of this quilt."*

Understanding community

Many schools from pre-school to the university boast about the
"community" atmosphere that differentiates them from others yet,
most people involved in these programs have difficulty articulating
what that means. Several alumni from Alpha talked about their
belief in the importance of working together to sort out problems
recalling specific instances that indicated to me their understanding

of community values. One story told by an alumnus captures the spirit of community that was encouraged in Alpha. He said that one year "the annual trip was in jeopardy because several class rules had been violated the year before." Students were panicked about missing the trip and that "never before had the trip been canceled." He remembered, "this was upsetting, and as a class we asked the teachers if we could have a second chance and try and convince them that, indeed, we were responsible enough." The class officers decided to call a class meeting to discuss the issue; and the class moderator asked the teachers to leave the room. Although teachers were usually a part of class meetings, they agreed to let students discuss this issue without them. He described the meeting to me saying there was much discussion, "about an hour and a half worth where everyone spoke." As a class they comprised a list of "responsiblity" rules to present to teachers, each class member vowing they would be obeyed. Then someone went to get the teachers, and while they waited not a person spoke.

When the teachers entered the room the moderator placed them in the middle of our circle and explained what we had decided. He recalled, "still, no one but the moderator had spoken." In his memory the quiet was "deafening" until one by one each class member stood in place and spoke. Each student talked about responsibility and accountability and how he or she intended to make sure mistakes made during the past year were not repeated. He said they all spoke with emotion and conviction. I could still hear it in his voice as he was telling the story years later. By the time the third person had spoken a tissue box was being passed around, not only to most of the students but for the teachers as well. The teachers agreed with the rules put forth by the class, and planning for the trip continued.

This class meeting was the subject of several student stories because, I think, it demonstrated to them the power of community action where people come together, sort out differences, decide on a common goal and present a workable solution. What may be most significant about this event is the notion that students in Alpha actually believed they could influence the final outcome. They understood the principles of democratic governance, how to change a rule, and the procedure for overturning a decision. One student told me, "only in Alpha would teachers ever give their students that kind of a second chance, and only in Alpha would the whole class cry and it would be acceptable." Another student expressed the long-lasting emotional effects she and her friends felt from that incident saying they "still talk about that class meeting—you know the crying thing," and even though she was out of high school as she was telling me this, she said she "still gets a lump in her throat when it comes to that memory." Community was, indeed, created in Alpha.

Building community in Alpha involved sharing many experiences and connecting with class members in numerous ways. It also grew because students felt they were valued and essential parts of the classroom, as if their presence or absence made a difference to the organization. Alpha and community became synonymous concepts for many. When asked to name one characteristic essential to the working of Alpha, Carol replied, "community." Student stories revealed how much effort it took to keep a group functioning as they learned how valuable each member was to its growth. One student told how she came to understand community through her experiences in the program. She described this idea thusly:

> Before I became an Alpha student, I wasn't sure what "community" meant. I always thought that it had to be a whole town and no matter what, you were automatically a community. When I came to Alpha, I realized that you can't just call yourself one without putting some effort into trying to be close to the people in your town or at least be nice to them. When I call Alpha a community, I mean that we are a different kind of family in school and we all care for each other. There are a few things that you can put in words about how Alpha is a community, but a few you just have to figure out yourself. These are a few things that I think makes a community: working out differences in a respectful way, listening to each other's ideas and come out with a solution that satisfies everybody, and learn to listen to what everybody has to say.

Much of what was being heralded as best middle level practices in the early 1990s was seen in action in the Alpha classroom. The close "family-like" atmosphere maintained throughout the middle school years modeled the movement's advocacy for long-term relationships with students. The close connections among and between students and teachers mirrored the community atmosphere necessary for democratic living. I saw Alpha students talking over concerns with each other, working out problems, and discussing each other's hopes, desires, fears, and worries. The organization of the curriculum allowed these rich discussions and connected the skills and content of the disciplines to a "bigger more personal idea."

> *Much of what was being heralded as best*
> *middle level practices in the early 1990s*
> *was seen in action in the Alpha classroom.*

While content-focused activities may give students knowledge, Alpha's classroom structure built on democratic principles of caring about ideas, things, and each other, gave students skills as well as knowledge to handle situations that come up in their daily lives.

The strength of any community is often measured by how its members respond to threats from outside pressures and internal events that disrupt its harmony. Alpha members have stood strong through various outside challenges to its organization and curriculum presented in the 70s and 80s. But, many class members told me, a tragedy within the classroom was the toughest test of all. It happened one day as a student reached for a book high on a shelf and the bookcase fell directly on her, knocking her unconscious. Students in the room at the time remember the "shock" they felt as they heard the "crash." They say they still vividly hear that sound years later. One girl said when she realized what had happened to her friend, Alyssia, her "heart felt like it weighed 12 pounds." During the weeks that followed while Alyssia lay unconscious in the hospital, members of the class spent time doing "little else than talking about the incident." They questioned, spoke, listened, yelled, cried. The conversations, in pairs, small groups, and as a whole class, ranged from discussing what had happened on that day to thinking about their friend. And when Alyssia died, discussions turned to ones of purpose and connections. Students wondered about how the life of a friend could be cut short; others regretted they didn't know her better. These conversations were encouraged by teachers and the professionals called in to work with the class. Some were structured for full class participation; most were held informally among students, and between teachers and students as they tried to sort out their emotions. Many students told me how they wanted to stay in class with their friends during these weeks—Alpha acting as a "cocoon" protecting them from the realities of death. They pulled together through these days, holding on to each other for support. One student claimed, "we became an even closer community than before. We learned how important everybody in the class is..." There is some irony in the fact that the first unit for the class that year had been on life's beginnings, looking at origins of birth and the initial stages of development. I had a sense of the curriculum coming full circle as students told me about their experiences with life's ending. ☆

I know they believe in me and care about how I'm doing academically. And I think, because of that, I try to work harder for them and end up learning more. — a sixth grader

V

The Core of Education

5. *To encourage the formation of an intellectually curious and creative being, well grounded in basic knowledge and ready to apply it to a field of learning far beyond the usual.*

—Fifth objective of program, adopted 1971

What is the core of the middle level experience, its center of gravity? Many middle school leaders point to its organization—interdisciplinary teams, student-teacher advisories. Teachers believe it's the match that is important—pairing content with student needs. Students say their friends and classmates matter most. For an observer of the Alpha Program peeking in regularly from the outside, it is clear that learning is at the center; it is reflected in students' faces around the classroom. Working with friends, one student as inquisitive as the next, doing things never thought possible, all actively struggling toward that moment when they say, "I got it!!" That's what is at the center of the middle school experience in Alpha.

Middle school organization and interdisciplinary teaching—Some history

By the early 1990s, the middle school movement had taken a firm hold in Vermont as many districts moved to establish a 5-8 or 6-8 grade level component alongside the elementary and secondary levels. This change meant more than reconfiguring classrooms; it meant trying to change the way instruction is conducted. As the single subject, single grade junior high model began to diminish, different classroom organizations emerged.

At the middle school in Shelburne, the principal initiated conversations with the entire faculty around ideas of curricular reform and working together on teams. He arranged for faculty members to spend time exploring the possibility of interdisciplinary teams within all classrooms in the school. There was limited teacher support for any change in the beginning. But with gentle prodding from John Winton, along with conversations about research findings supporting such changes, the "theme" approach to the study of a topic began to take hold, focusing on small units of study that included more than two content areas. By the end of 1990 all teachers, including special area teachers in the school, were organized into three groups, Humanities, Technology, and Communication, in order to pursue ideas in an interdisciplinary way. Teams decided on a topic to explore within their area and met with a group of students twice a week for a total of 80 minutes to investigate a topic. This "exploratory time," as it was called, was the beginning for teachers in "regular" classrooms in Shelburne to work together across content disciplines. It challenged the single discipline thinking of several teachers, and some of them found working closely with others was difficult.

Teachers found interdisciplinary teaming, even for a short time each week, difficult because it required commitment and responsibility to each other that went beyond what they were used to in their departmental specialization. They had to see themselves as team members first and subject-matter specialists second. Although theory said that students would benefit from this organization because content would be connected and therefore more meaningful, many were skeptical. The organizing centers would provide unity and coherence to the content studied. Also while working together, teachers and students would share not only academic but social and emotional needs, getting to know one another more closely than in a regular classroom situation. Interpersonal bonds would be built between members of the group as they engaged in learning activities. And working with colleagues would enhance teachers' knowledge and skills—at least that was what teachers in Shelburne were told.

While the theory was interesting, even somewhat exciting to some at the middle school, in practice it fell short. After a few weeks of implementing "exploratory time" it became obvious that establishing an effective group environment required more from teachers than agreeing on a topic to study. They needed skills they did not have. They realized teaching together required them to collaborate, share decision making, compromise, and rely on and trust each other. When looking back, teachers said they were unprepared for the collaboration that was necessary. Weekly team meetings became longer because it took time to incorporate everyone's thoughts and ideas into a theme that could be studied. They said that while they debated topics to study they also had to grapple with broader considerations about philosophical issues such as the "role of cooperation in teaching and learning."

At these meetings teachers sorted through issues involved with working together such as how to communicate effectively with each other and operate efficiently with the whole group. They wondered to themselves—and often aloud to each other—if the outcomes were worth the effort. They questioned whether these discussions about working together were a good use of planning time. "Shouldn't there be more focus on content?" they asked. Teachers said they had to prepare for their regular daily classes, and there was limited time for planning them. As I listened to them discuss the move to teaming I heard their frustration. Some were hesitant to try something different; they seemed reluctant to move out of a structure that had worked well for them in the past. However, this move to limited teaming, 80 minutes a week, was the start of a different conversation between teachers at the school. Topics at meetings switched from discussions of logistics (who goes where when) to ones of appropriate objectives and content relevance. Perhaps this is exactly the move John Winton had in mind when he began this process.

> *With the introduction of limited interdisciplinary teaching in the entire school, the curricular organization of the Alpha Program moved closer to that of the rest of the school.*

Alpha assumes new status

With the introduction of limited interdisciplinary teaching in the entire school, the curricular organization of the Alpha Program moved closer to that of the rest of the school. Teachers in "regular" classrooms began to notice the way the Alpha teachers talked together while planning activities; they asked them questions about designing interdisciplinary units of study. The principal encouraged the formation of team identities by using Alpha as an example and a promise of more resources as an incentive. He told me "Alpha was the first class to get a full-time teacher's aide." Other teachers came to him and asked, "how come Alpha's got an aide?" He said he told them "because they work together cooperatively and that makes different demands on their time." Hoping to encourage other teachers to work more closely together he said to them "look, if you want to work together cooperatively, then form a team and begin to develop a program that would require support." This was not easy for some teachers. They had neither the experience nor the desire to work closely with others. They especially didn't like the idea that in order to receive more resources they would have to change how they were teaching.

Teachers from regular classrooms believed the Alpha program was the curricular model favored by the administration, and they had some problems with perceived favoritism. Many objected to the open, flexible structure of the program, continuing to wonder if students were learning what they needed to succeed beyond the middle grades. They also were concerned about the role of the teacher in such a setting. It appeared to them that Alpha teachers were generalists, encouraging students to explore and discover across many areas of study, missing depth in any area. They saw themselves as specialists, experts in a discipline. They felt knowledgeable in their specialty and competent to direct student inquiries in a particular subject. The reason most often told to me for objecting to interdisciplinary study was its questionable effect on student learning. Another objection not explicitly stated but somewhere close to the surface I felt, was that some teachers feared loss of identity with this change. They liked the specialist status given them by being the history, language arts, math expert and fought against giving up that status. While teachers agreed to try the interdisciplinary approach for two periods a week, they did so because this time was exploratory, non-essential. Content remained the sacred text and discipline-specific classes remained the focus of their teaching. This argument seems rather outmoded now looking back from a period when interdisciplinary teaming is prevalent in many middle schools, but these teachers represented the thinking that was common at that time.

The difficulty with choice

Family choice in classrooms had been available in Shelburne since the opening of the school. Parents liked having a say in which teachers their children would have for the year, and they selected certain ones for a variety reasons, not always having to do with philosophical agreement about learning. For the most part the families who chose Alpha did so because they believed in the type of learning presented by its structure and organization. This was certainly the case in the beginning years of the program. During the later 1980s, when the program had existed for 15 years and was well-known in the community, some families put their children in Alpha less for agreement with the philosophy and more for practical or personal reasons. Explanations given to me ranged from parent perceptions of fewer demands for performance—an attractive characteristic for some parents of fourth-grade children—to more freedom to move about, to better teachers than available in a specific grade level classroom, in other words, a way to avoid an undesirable teacher.

The result of this flexible policy was that children sometimes were placed in Alpha for only a year or two to accommodate family wishes. Therefore, the makeup of the classroom fluctuated yearly, making it difficult to establish a community feeling. The administration moved families in and out regularly if deemed necessary. This meant some years there were many fourth-graders and few eighth-graders in Alpha; the next year the numbers might be reversed. There were years when aides to students with special challenges increased the number of adults present in the room and years when two teachers were the only adults.

The team of students and teachers representing Alpha also varied in size depending on demand. It moved from 75 students with three teachers to 50 students with two teachers to over 100 students with a teaching team of four. In the midst of class-size changes and various room locations from 1973 through 1988, two teachers, Carol and Warren, with one instructional aide, provided the stability necessary to maintain the continuity of the multiage, integrated curricular organization. And when Warren left to care for his aging parents and work in the family business in 1989, Carol became the mainstay, the bearer of the Alpha vision. Additional teachers came and went during the next 15 years—Rich Jesset, Dick Garnet, Linda Mann, Kris Spengler, Jeanne Cota, Cyndy Hall, Meg Kenney, Than James—each leaving something of himself or herself in Alpha, a certain spin that influenced parts of the program; but Carol provided the constant filtering of ideas that was needed to maintain and strengthen the program for the years ahead.

The role of the principal during this time of flux and change in Shelburne was important. John recognized the cultural context in which the Shelburne Middle School was bound. He was aware of emerging research that called for reorganizing the school and the curriculum around best middle level practice, and he said he saw much of that in the Alpha Program; but he alo understood the resistance to change felt by an experienced teaching staff and some parents. He admitted

> I had hoped that Alpha would continue to grow and grow, but we had to depend upon the parents and the teachers. It never snowballed. There were some parents who had a very different view, and that had to be respected. They wanted a very structured, 'tell my kid what to do and when to do it' kind of classroom.

Faculty discussions during these years resulted in two curricular options for families, one associated with discipline specific classrooms whose members regrouped to explore a theme two periods during the week and Alpha, a multiage, integrated curricular program. Although teachers had made a slight shift towards changing their practice, the distinction between "regular" and "Alpha" remained. While John viewed the school somewhat futuristically, he realized the demands of such a vision. After 20 years of service to the community he retired. In his years in Shelburne he oversaw the construction of a school, set in place curricular options that moved teachers toward thinking about interdisciplinary work, supported the integrated Alpha classroom, and planted seeds for teaming. Community and school personnel praised his leadership in providing Shelburne with the first school in Vermont dedicated to middle level learning; its citizens, parents, teachers, and community members would ultimately determine what that would mean.

Of all the programs I knew of in my years as an administrator for the middle grades, the Alpha program came the closest to serving the unique needs of young adolescents as first outlined when junior high schools were established in the beginning of the last century. Alpha provided a creative structure for bringing out the best in both students and teachers.

—*John Winton, 2004*

A new era begins—time of change

With the retirement of Principal Winton and the hiring of a new principal in 1989, the push toward middle level organization and practice became even more pronounced. The new principal, Dr. Carol Spencer, was hired in part for her commitment to and experience with middle level philosophy. Previously she had been a principal in a small school in Vermont where she helped implement a new organizational structure. She told me her agreement with, and mandate from, the school board in Shelburne on her hire was to move the school further in the direction of the middle level philosophy outlined by the newly published Carnegie Foundation's Report (1989), *Turning Points: Preparing American Youth for the Twenty-First Century*. The findings in this report pointed out that early adolescence is a particularly vulnerable time for developing at-risk behaviors; kids need greater support during these years than at other times in their schooling. This report recommended having teacher teams work in flexible curriculum blocks. Three or four teachers would comprise a team that shared responsibility for a group of youngsters. This organization would allow ongoing communication among the teachers creating a sense of responsibility and caring for each individual student. In Shelburne, movement toward this vision started with the "exploratory" groupings established by the previous administration. Principal Spencer's task was to attempt to institute this curricular direction for the academic courses. The superintendent of the Chittenden South Supervisory District at the time, Bill Crocoll, was known for his futurist thinking. He outlined a vision for the entire consolidated district including Shelburne, which endorsed many of the recommendations found in the Carnegie Report. It was the guide Carol Spencer used as she began the task of reorganizing the Shelburne School.

The changes envisioned by Superintendent Crocoll were outlined in a notebook titled *The Transformation Process* which was endorsed by the district's administrators. In it he described an individualized learning environment for all students, one where they could progress at their own rate and design their own learning opportunities. The use of technology was central to the implementation of this plan both to expand learning possibilities and register and maintain records. Two schools in the union district already had endorsed this vision publicly through their school mission statements; three other schools, Shelburne among them, were working toward that end. The Shelburne Board of Director's clear directive as understood by Carol was to "develop a vision statement for the middle school that matched the vision articulated by Dr. Crocoll." She told me she realized rather quickly this was a "complex and complicated task."

When Carol arrived she found the school curriculum in somewhat of a state of disarray. There was little agreement among the teachers about the organizational structures that were in place. With John's departure some teachers and community members began to speak publicly against any interdisciplinary work (a reaction to "exploratory time") and for a move to ability tracking and single-subject classes. Carol found that some teachers adopted a "wait and see" attitude viewing the changes initiated by John as "experimental." They told her the variations proposed seemed "reasonable in theory" but questioned the effectiveness with a classroom of 25 students. And there was Alpha, which appeared to exemplify the vision set forth by Superintendent Crocoll except for the emphasis on technology. The Shelburne School was behind others in the district in the area of technology, and none of the classrooms had either the hardware or the personnel support to make technology a central part of student learning. Carol noticed during her first months in Shelburne there had been little talk among faculty and staff about the principles or advantages of the "transformation process" which had been mandated by the district administrators.

The reality of the workload for teachers at this time, as told to me by Principal Carol and confirmed by teachers, was that in "regular" classrooms they were working with approximately 180 students throughout the week. Since they remained departmentalized by grade, they shared students for academic core areas every day, and then on Tuesday and Thursday afternoons during Exploratory Time they worked with an entirely different group of students. Teachers appeared exhausted and, Carol said when she interviewed them at the beginning of her tenure, she found them to be "caring and accountable people who knew they were not being the least bit effective in any part of their teaching life." They told her they were not "being answerable to their core kids" because they had too many of them (140) and they described the interdisciplinary time as "a series of fun activities not connected to other learning." Carol told me that under these circumstances it wasn't too hard to bring people together to discuss a different organizational plan. Teachers were ready for a different structure, and many of them wanted a return to the old system.

A model emerges

As a new principal, Carol spent time in each of the classrooms trying to understand the "life of the school." The new principal walked into Alpha to spend a few hours and ended up staying three full days working with students. During these days she went from somebody who couldn't see it to somebody who could never step foot in another regular classroom without saying "wait a minute." What she saw in those three days was revolutionary for her. She claims it "opened windows of possibilities about children and what they could be taught in school settings as nothing ever had in my entire personal life and childhood, college degrees, or previous principalships, nothing. Finally I understood what learning was and what it could be."

> *The new principal walked into Alpha to spend a few hours and ended up staying three full days working with students. What she saw was revolutionary for her.*

Carol describes what she saw in one way as "messy." Students were all working on different activities. While some were reading quietly, others were constructing things on a table; still others were practicing for a play. "Nothing seemed to go together." She heard students arguing, persuading, negotiating, mediating. She saw them listening to each other and explaining their ideas in various ways. She says she talked with students, questioned teachers and observed activities, trying to understand what was happening, "letting meaning evolve." After three days in the classroom she concluded "...the only way to really mean every child must learn is to find a system such as this that allows students to learn at their own pace, in their own way." She watched them choose materials to use and structure their own time. She observed how they reacted intellectually and emotionally to this responsibility and heard them take time to process the problems along the way. Reflecting on her own schooling she told me she had never attended a school where she didn't "sit in seats in rooms, including doctoral seminars." What she saw here was an active, noisy classroom where students moved about at will, talking and laughing as they learned. It became a model for her to use to implement the ideas set forth in the district's plan for transformation.

> ### *Alpha gives you the tools to learn.*
> ### *It's a university setting on a 5-8*
> ### *grade level.* —Alpha graduate

Carol says that after her time in Alpha she wondered how she would get teachers in other classrooms to move toward the vision set forth by the district. She had learned from previous experience with reorganizing schools that the most effective way for teachers to change what they do in their rooms is to involve them in the process of change. She, therefore, formed the Transformed Study School Group (TSSG), with faculty representatives from all grades. Their job was to take the vision set forth by the district and form it to fit the context of Shelburne. She said to them "We've got to stop pretending that we know what this (transformed school) is, and we have to start defining it." The TSSG set about gathering information, inviting speakers to talk about recent research in learning that proposed new organizational structures for schools. Visitors from other schools presented their experience with restructuring curricular goals; Superintendent Crocoll articulated further for them his vision of a transformed school; the teachers from Alpha showed the group how they used the district's *Essential Learning Behaviors* document to design learning objectives and goals.

This period of study and investigation was a pivotal point of exposure for the Alpha curriculum to the rest of the school and the district. Even though many teachers had taught side-by-side with the Alpha program throughout the years, most of them had little real knowledge of how the learning process was being carried out in the classroom or understood how it was tied to broader goals and objectives. They only knew what happened in that room was "different" from what they were doing. Those committee members who were open to change listened to what the Alpha teachers said and took new interest in the process. The teachers from Alpha who were members of the TSSG articulated clearly the logistical functioning of the program and the reasons for its structure. The years of working through pressures to conform to traditional standards had made them "strong in their convictions about what it means to learn and what it means to teach."

A common mission

For two years, 1990-92, the TSSG met and worked on a vision statement and articulation of learning outcomes for students in the Shelburne school that would align with the school board's mandate and the vision set by Superintendent Crocoll. The final document, endorsed by the staff with a few dissenting opinions, read:

> It is the mission of the Shelburne School District to ensure that each child investigates, masters, and applies the knowledge, skills, values, and behaviors necessary for lifelong learning and meaningful participation in a global society.

In addition to the general mission statement they outlined learning goals, called *Essential Behaviors*, to be used as guides in planning activities and assessing student progress and growth. These Essential Behaviors stated that to be an effective learner one must:

- Think creatively and critically
- Communicate effectively
- Cooperate with others
- Use appropriate resources to seek, access, and apply knowledge
- Function independently
- Take risks to succeed
- Exhibit self-confidence in learning
- Create options and make choices

The articulation of these processes as foundational to learning for students in Shelburne was a noted departure from previous goals that said the accumulation of knowledge was most important. The *Essential Behaviors* document was in line with the principles presented in the 1985 Carnegie document *Turning Points* for the education of middle-level students. It closely matched the processes outlined in the philosophy statements for the Alpha program that called for giving students the skills and support "to encourage the formation of an intellectually curious and creative being." The communication of these behaviors at this time changed the focus of learning from the subject-specific content to processes where students exhibited ways of approaching, investigating, and questioning knowledge. Emphasis switched from the "what" of learning to the "how"—from content outcomes to process ones. With the presentation of this document the TSSG began the process of curricular reform in the school. Implementation of the vision statement and learning behaviors into daily activities in classrooms would be more difficult.

> *As principal, Carol Spencer augmented the move toward curricular revision by proposing that all students and teachers organize into three teams that included three grades, 6, 7, 8.*

As principal, Carol Spencer augmented the move toward curricular revision by proposing that all students and teachers organize into three teams that included three grades, 6, 7, 8. Her thinking was that this structural change would facilitate discussions among teachers about multiage groupings and cross-discipline curriculum; it would be difficult for teachers to remain exclusively within separate subject areas. During the 91-92 school year, teachers agreed to try this "teaming" as long as they had a say in how they were organized and who they worked alongside. Even teachers who provided the "specials" (living arts, art, music) became members of a team. The teams chose names, *Opportunity. Excellence,* and of course, *Alpha.* Carol equalized the budget process by putting the same dollars behind each student and giving teams control of their spending parameters.

The following two years, 1993 and 1994, were full of faculty discussions and professional development activities for the faculty at Shelburne Middle School. Consultants were brought in to work with teachers and the board, helping them understand what needed to be done to align classroom activities with the goals and objectives of the district; newly formed teams were given time to plan and learn how to work together; staff members were encouraged to attend professional development seminars and conferences that emphasized areas of curricular reform. A concerted effort was made by the administration to involve faculty and staff in the process of change that had started with a district mandate and was articulated through the school vision.

As newly formed teams struggled to define themselves, the teaching team in Alpha was a model.

During this time the distinction between the Alpha program and the rest of the school became somewhat blurred. As newly formed teams struggled to define themselves, the teaching team in Alpha was a model. They had established an identity. Instead of being labeled "the alternative" classroom, the Alpha program became just one multiage curricular option offered to families in Shelburne. Other teams now had the opportunity to organize in ways that had been characteristic of Alpha, establishing a community atmosphere, controlling scheduling, making independent curricular and budgetary decisions, and measuring student progress over three years. Some teachers embraced this reorganization seeing it as a chance to move toward a more integrated model of learning; others were skeptical, wondering if students would come out of eighth grade prepared for future studies at the secondary school; still others opposed the change outright—"Alpha is Alpha and we're not that." Although as a whole the faculty wanted relief from the large number of students they had been working with, some teachers were disgruntled with the direction the change was taking.

The struggle with change
Several teachers told me they thought the vision statement they had adopted seemed rather harmless at the time it was adopted. The goal of providing students with knowledge, skills, and dispositions

necessary for leading enriching lives was a worthy one. There was little argument with that. However, interpretation of its meaning was more complex. When the board of directors pushed teachers to demonstrate the implementation of the vision in written goals and objectives, questions and discontent began to surface; and when the statement was made available to the community at large, objections were raised: Which skills? Whose values? What kind of participation in society? And how is global defined? Challenges to the new direction for curricular activities put forth by the principal and the TSSG surfaced from many areas but were felt most intensely within the school itself at the teacher level. Change had come quickly to Shelburne. In two years, a new vision statement had been adopted; all classrooms had been reconfigured to multiage groupings; teachers were paired with colleagues to work on teams.

Carol Spencer believed that the changes proposed in Shelburne during these years were supported by research studies whose findings emphasized the importance of process as well as content. Each component of the mission statement and the *Essential Behaviors Document* was supported by research studies. She also believed these changes were called for by the changing demands of young adolescents. The world of the adolescent in 1994 was comprised of powers and perspectives seldom thought of 20 years before and not at all when their parents were young. During the 1990s life for 10- to 14-year-olds consisted of computers, video games, and music, with the entire planet accessible through television, satellites, and air travel. With the glut of information we now have, she said, thought can be chaotic and even dangerous. Her point was that to deal with a rapidly changing world a different structure was required if schools were to help students sort out the complexity of their lives. As I thought about what she said I realized the changes in the way and means of learning that had taken place over two decades. Whereas learning had once demanded from students a good memory and the ability to sit through lectures, it now involved learning how to find new solutions to old problems, discovering ways to make decisions and commitments, figuring out how to work together with people sometimes not in the same classroom or town. The advent of the digital revolution made old ways of knowing obsolete. Adjusting to the new organizational structures posed a threat to normalcy for teachers in Shelburne.

The newly proposed interdisciplinary organization also ran contrary to the notion of schooling held by some parents and community members.

The newly proposed interdisciplinary organization also ran contrary to the notion of schooling held by some parents and community members who read about these changes in the weekly newspaper where school board meetings were reported. For the most part community members not directly involved in the school had no understanding of the changes that were needed or the school's responsibility for addressing these demands. Several community members talked to me about their concerns that emphasizing process over content would not prepare their children for the next level of education or the level beyond that. In their view, the most important purpose of school was to transmit information about the world. They knew "school" from their own experience as places where learning content dominated. They feared substance learning would be neglected with the new school structure. In addition, with the move to three-year teams for all students and teachers, families saw the previously valued option of yearly "choice" in curricular models would be lost. As the attendance at school board meetings grew, so did community skepticism about the changes that had taken place. Amidst discussions in several contexts, contrary at times, the direction from the school board to the principal, as Carol Spencer told me, remained steady—continue to work for a common vision for the school that embraced the ideas set forth by the district and the superintendent.

Alpha's move to the mainstream

Alpha made a conscious decision to align itself organizationally with the rest of the school during this time of change. Until then it had been a five-year program spanning grades four through eight. With the formation of three-year teams throughout the school, Alpha considered splitting into two teams, one for fourth and fifth grade students and another for six- through eighth-grade students. There was much discussion about this possibility. The teachers saw some advantages, "offering Alpha the opportunity to be full partners with the rest of the school" in goals and structure. Students, on the other hand, liked the different structure of Alpha and worried that the change meant "they were going to be like everyone else; it wouldn't be unique."

Parents, involved with the program in the late 80s and early 90s, told me this change was a "crucial one for the direction of the program." They said they were apprehensive about maintaining a sense of community, wondering if it could evolve as strongly in three years as it had in five. Over five years they had seen their children develop a "sense of responsibility" to themselves, each other, and the program, and they were concerned that teachers might not "get to know the students as well" and, as a consequence, "learning might suffer." Some parents told me that they wondered if three years was enough time, as one parent put it, "to establish the classroom as a safe place to learn where risks would be taken and failures worked through."

Administrators at the school told me they felt the structure in Alpha lent "credibility to the idea that education doesn't just happen in one year." They argued this was an opportunity to build "cogency within the system school-wide" that would benefit Alpha as well as align it with other teams. They told those in Alpha opposed to the three-year structure that it would actually "allow the practice of Alpha to grow." At the end of all the discussions, it was decided to split the Alpha program into two groups, allying itself with the newly organized middle school teams throughout the rest of the school.

During 1991 and 1992 school year two of the Alpha teachers remained with the sixth- through eighth-grade team and one of the Alpha teachers, with a new partner, created the fourth- through fifth-grade component from which students could advance into Alpha after the fifth grade. The transition to this structure was tricky. There were students who had started in the five-year Alpha program as fourth graders who left during their fifth grade year because of the split and returned to Alpha the following year. The switch in teachers and structure (they went from youngest to oldest to youngest) was confusing for them. Carol Smith, as the teacher with the most experience and understanding of philosophy, was instrumental to the success of the split. Once again, she provided the stabilizing force, helping students and parents with the transition, bringing teachers from both classrooms together to collaborate on activities, leading the Alpha program from its alternative status to its more mainstreamed position.

Carol Smith's knowledge about learning and her classroom skills moved her to a lead position not only in the curriculum discussions at school but in the state of Vermont where, prompted by the national standards movement of the early 1990s, broad-based discussions of educational goals had begun. Several people described to me the characteristics that made Carol a leader. They said she was an enthusiastic reader of the emerging middle school literature who studied research findings and was a keen observer of practice. Describing Carol's work to me the principal said, "If there's anything that woman has brought to the profession, it's a pride in being able to look at good research and good practice and adapt and adopt absolutely anything...if it works for kids, she's willing to adapt it and adopt it." Her passion and dedication to student learning was evident throughout her work in the school. She argued at faculty meetings about the mismatch between what she saw as current classroom practices and learning needs. Committee minutes indicate that during these years she spoke passionately on best middle level teaching practice and emphasized the importance of stable long-term relationships between teachers and students, the necessity of connecting principles and concepts across disciplines, and the value of joint participation by all members of a group in achieving learning goals. I heard her articulate quite powerfully to community members at school board meetings the importance of the child-classroom fit for successful learning to occur.

When Carol was selected Vermont's Teacher of the Year, the entire Alpha team accompanied her to receive the award from Governor Howard Dean.

In 1995, Carol was elected Vermont's Teacher of the Year, an award given to one teacher in every state who made significant contributions to the field of education. This award moved her and the Alpha Program into the limelight of the educational community at the state level. The statewide teacher journal said of her, "Carol Smith, as the standard bearer for what is unique and best in Vermont public schools, is a choice the entire educational community in Vermont can celebrate." With her interest in involving students in the process of learning, it is no surprise that the entire Alpha class accompanied her to the state capital to receive the award.

Student learning at the core

Student involvement in curriculum development had always been a part of Alpha; however, following Carol's attendance at a summer curriculum workshop directed by Jim Beane in 1990, the degree of it increased. Alpha began using the process advocated by Beane that involved all students and faculty in selecting units for study. During the first week of school the class gathered in a large group to plan the themes for the year. The process began with teachers asking students two questions: "What questions or concerns do you have about yourself?" "What questions or concerns do you have about the world?" Working with peers in smaller groups, students listed their responses, prioritized their choices, and presented their top ones to the entire class for discussion. At the end of the discussion, students were asked to vote on the choices presented. In this way curriculum was created, as Beane suggests, from the "bottom up." Students were able to lobby for a topic of personal interest that often became the community area of study. Students saw their interests incorporated into a larger context. Beane, whose influential book *The Middle School Curriculum: From Rhetoric to Reality* (1990) came out that fall, subsequently visited Alpha on two occasions.

Carol's selection as Vermont's Teacher of the Year brought recognition to Alpha for having pushed the curriculum parameters even further. In the Alpha room students linked their own interests with a larger social world. The curricular themes studied in Alpha became more problem and issue centered, broad enough to use with varied activities and involve knowledge without regard for subject or disciplinary lines. Clearly, students liked being involved. One student told me she felt "trusted." Another reported, "having a part in deciding curricular topics was a wonderful experience that allowed me to be myself through a tough time in every girl's life, adolescence."

Students also learned to take a more active role at the other end of the learning process, participating in the assessment of what they had learned. Student-led parent conferences gave them the responsibility for documenting and explaining their progress toward learning goals that they had set for themselves. Twice a year they held conferences with their parents where they talked about the studies. It was a task not taken lightly by the students. They worked steadily throughout the month before the conference organizing their work into folders to present to their parents. As an observer of conferences, I saw several groups of students with their parents, sitting in small chairs in various parts of the room. Folders were open on desks displaying work; students talked confidently about the progress they had made toward reaching their goals; parents listened intently asking questions and probing for further explanations.

> *Student-led parent conferences*
> *gave them the responsibility for*
> *documenting and explaining their*
> *progress toward learning goals that*
> *they had set for themselves*

Teachers moved quietly around the room monitoring the process, helping students retrieve work from places around the room where it was displayed, answering questions posed by parents. I saw students who were clearly in charge of the situation. They discussed effectively successes and challenges they had met in their work. After their explanations were finished, with their parent's help, they set new learning goals for the next semester.

Student-directed conferences required students to do a good deal of reflective self-evaluation about learning and the work they attempted and completed. It also helped them develop skills in communication. One teacher captured its strength when she described the process to me as "an incredibly rich system that honors children's voices through learning, what these students want their next steps to be, and what they think they're good at and why." Students told me they gained confidence in their ability to talk about what they learned as they organized their material for the conferences. One former student described the anxiety she felt about this activity during her first year in Alpha. She recalled, "the first time I presented my portfolio to my parents I was so nervous. It was the first time I was responsible for explaining what and how I had learned. I was terrified that I'd make some big mistake!" She went on to say that in the end "it went pretty well, my parents got to see all my work, and I got to talk about what I know most about, me." Her emerging confidence in explaining her learning was evident when she told me that by her last year in Alpha she was arguing with her parents about "why such and such was a reasonable goal given the other things I had accomplished." Some parents did have difficulty getting used to this type of conference. Some of them wanted more input from teachers and kept asking them to join the discussion. Once they realized their children were able to respond to their concerns and could explain everything, parents' focus switched from teacher to student as expert. I saw students speaking in calm, firm voices to their parents about the work they had done, confidently displaying their accomplishments, convincing them that they had made progress. In the eyes of students doing this for the first time I saw pleas to be listened to and believed. As they had more experience with the approach their look was steady and determined while they persuaded their parents of their abilities.

By 1992 students were positioned at the center of all activities in the Alpha Program.

By 1992 students were positioned at the center of all activities in the Alpha Program. They assumed responsibility for explaining their learning and the Alpha philosophy to others outside the classroom and school. Whereas previously the Alpha teachers had talked to interested groups about how the program worked, students now began to speak at local and regional meetings. For some students this new involvement pushed their skills further than they thought they could go; it gave them confidence as thinkers, explainers, and presenters. When presenting at the New England League of Middle Schools Conference (NELMS) one year a student described to me her fright at standing in front of teachers yet her sense of pride as she spoke fondly and confidently about Alpha. Another student told me "public speaking and communicating orally were never my forté." She told me this story:

*My brain had always tended to be a little bit in front
of my mouth, and I wasn't very comfortable in front of
people; so for my first couple of years in the program
I managed to let myself slide in this regard. The fall
of sixth grade sticks out in my mind because it was
then, at the NELMS conference, that I finally made a
breakthrough and confronted this fear. The workshop
for middle school teachers was held in Cape Cod,
and Than James took a group of us down to present.
My topic was "goals," and I remember sitting there
in front of a room full of teachers and just thinking,
"Can I really do this?" An hour after the session, after
speaking more or less cohesively, I knew that though
I was by no means perfect, the answer, of course, was
yes—I could (and did) do it. Not only was this a big
confidence boost, but also I realized that not being
good at something isn't a reason to avoid the area, but
rather a reason to pursue improvement in it.*

Students assumed new roles in the classroom as they became more central to the activities in Alpha. They were acquirers of knowledge, yes, but also planners, assessors, and explainers. Although Alpha now resembled the rest of the school in organization and multigrade level teams, it continued to distinguish itself by focusing on students as the designers of curriculum and as directors of their own learning.

Change comes slowly

Although most teachers in Shelburne had voted in favor of the vision set forth by the TSSG and welcomed the classroom structures that were in place, the move to multiyear, interdisciplinary teams by all teachers at the middle school level was difficult. Teachers continued to see themselves as subject-matter specialists first and team members second, a common hazard to successful teaming. Planning time, now done with others, often was devoted to teachers defending the amount of time students would need to spend doing subject specific lessons. They felt that boundaries had been blurred with the formation of interdisciplinary groups and worried about the amount of content students would receive. At the first team meeting the social studies teacher argued for two hours about history lessons while the language arts teacher made a case for literature study. Each believed the emphasis on the interdisciplinary structure would short-change certain areas of study. They wanted to be responsible only for the content of the subject they knew. Several teachers told me they did not see how they could assist students in learning a topic not in their area of study. In actuality what was happening, I inferred from observations and conversations with teachers, was that rather than fight the structure itself, teachers carved out their discipline identities within the framework of a team. They were encouraged to do so by some members of the community, those who did not fully understand the proposed structure and others who disagreed with it and wanted "specialists not generalists" in the classroom. The board of directors continued to mandate movement toward a common vision for the school that included teams of teachers working with students spanning three-year grade levels. Teachers stayed in their team, some rather begrudgingly so, for four years. The performance review of Principal Spencer during 1996 indicated that she was "not moving quickly enough" toward the vision. She told me she felt "caught in the turbulence of change."

In the spring of 1996, as an attempt to respond to the varying pressures and demands for school organization, Carol and the staff reorganized themselves again, this time into four teams, each spanning a three-year grade spread. The names of the teams were *Excellence, Cornerstone, Delta,* and *Alpha.* Each represented a different curricular model.

The Excellence team adapted a conventional single-subject approach common in most junior high schools. Each teacher taught his or her own content to a common group of students. For example, the math teacher on the team taught separate classes to sixth, seventh, and eighth graders. Students rotated among teachers and classes. Members of this team said that the difference for them from previous years was that they interacted with "a smaller number of students," teaching only those assigned to Excellence, and that was "a huge improvement." Team meetings consisted mainly of discussions about student progress mostly from a subject perspective.

The Cornerstone team also provided a single-discipline, single-grade approach but decided to incorporate thematic units to the content. General themes picked by the teaching team provided linking threads to the core content classes. Students studied the "Westward Movement of the American Frontier" in grade-level language arts, science, social studies, and math classes for example.

The Cornerstone team attempted to offer some coherence to the content by studying the same information from different discipline perspectives.

Members of the Delta team organized themselves around units of study that offered a blended model of curricular activities. Sixth, seventh, eighth graders were grouped by grade level for the core classes, math, science, language arts, social studies, and came together across grade levels for studies of particular topics like "change" or "democracy." This resembled the "exploratory" time initiated in previous years. The difficulty with this model was that the units of study had little connection with each other or with what was being covered in the discipline-specific classes. There was little unity among topics studied.

And then there was Alpha. It remained a multiyear, fully integrated curricular team. These four teams functioned through the 1996-97 school year. As each team took on its own identity and became more vocal about its organization, the curricular differences between them grew. The common vision called for by the school board and the district became more elusive. During 1997 Carol began discussion about once more realigning teaching teams in an effort to move the curricular models closer to that called for in the vision statement. She says that this attempt might have "pushed the system further or faster than it wanted to go." It was this initiative that brought the smoldering controversies about curriculum structure and classroom organization to the forefront.

> *Community pressure encouraged by the results of one survey indicated low support for the changes and sought a vote of "no confidence in the administration."*

A vocal group of parents, who thought that any teaming or multiage grouping was an attempt to move away from solid academic programming, turned several school board meetings into debates about how children learn and how they should be taught. One parent summarized his objections to interdisciplinary teaching by telling the local newspaper, "we didn't have confidence that the basics in math, spelling, grammar, and reading were being taught."

Several community forums, organized by the school board and administrators, were held to discuss the structural changes at the school and two town wide surveys were commissioned. Community pressure encouraged by the results of one survey indicated low support for the changes and sought a vote of "no confidence in the administration." It led to the resignation of Carol Spencer as principal in the fall of 1996. Thinking about that time a few years later with the advantage of hindsight and perspective, she told me that she realized Shelburne didn't get the support from the community to transform the whole system. She speculated that maybe she should have spent more time working with the community to convince citizens of the advantages of the reorganization. She says she had relied on the faculty and staff to do that and didn't realize that wasn't enough. In actuality some teachers aligned with community members in their objections. Carol told me that she felt she had tried to change too much at one time in Shelburne, but her driving force had been the board's directive to provide a common vision, which remained the directive until the day she resigned.

Effects of change

The Shelburne School was once again caught in the midst of confusion and turmoil. The superintendent stepped in to handle day-to-day operations for a time until an interim principal was hired to finish out the year. Teachers continued functioning on their teams the way they had defined these roles; the discussion at school board meetings intensified as board members tried to sort out disagreements about the best direction for the school. Listening to reports of these discussions and reading records of these meetings, it was clear to me that at this time Shelburne was a community divided; consensus on future direction seemed beyond reach at this time.

Throughout the remainder of that year and into the next, discussions about future directions continued at the classroom and community level. Arguments were disruptive, even hurtful at times, causing disputes among neighborhood friends and harsh words between colleagues. People took sides arguing a particular curricular model or calling for a "complete overhaul" of the school. Teachers did not want to go through another organizational change so tried to "calm the waters" by supporting the status quo. Some of them told me, "we had carved out our niche in the school, let us do our jobs." They felt the distinctions between the teams were evident and clear; the common vision called for by the board could wait.

It is perhaps no irony that the tensions apparent in Shelburne at this time mirrored the struggle felt by the targets of that conflict, its middle school students. They were youth on the threshold of adolescence, struggling to "fit in" or "stand apart." Just like the students, members of the school community, faculty, staff and parents, were struggling with questions of acceptance and difference. The job of the board of directors in Shelburne was to decide what would be allowed and what would be rejected as part of the school's identity as an educational institution.

Alpha—figuring out a fit

The public discussions over how the school should be organized and children taught strengthened the commitment by the Alpha Program to its founding convictions. When defending their curricular activities at public meetings, Alpha teachers reaffirmed their belief in the curricular model that had developed, reiterating the original principles as the center of its purpose. They believed the student-directed curriculum that had evolved in Alpha had reached "a balance in activities" that offered enough academic rigor to meet the district criteria, enough innovation to keep students curious and learning exciting, and enough similarity with the rest of the school to stay aligned with the vision statement that had caused so much turmoil. Students and teachers in Alpha learned during the somewhat turbulent years of the 1990s how to stay part of a system in some areas and move beyond in others. At these public meetings where school goals and learning objectives were discussed, parents, teachers, and students of the Alpha community presented their views with a sense of confidence and assurance about their identity. In several ways these discussions made them more committed and dedicated as a group to the program's philosophy. Members of the Alpha team presented a program that had a sense of stability, balance, and even progress throughout these years. ☆

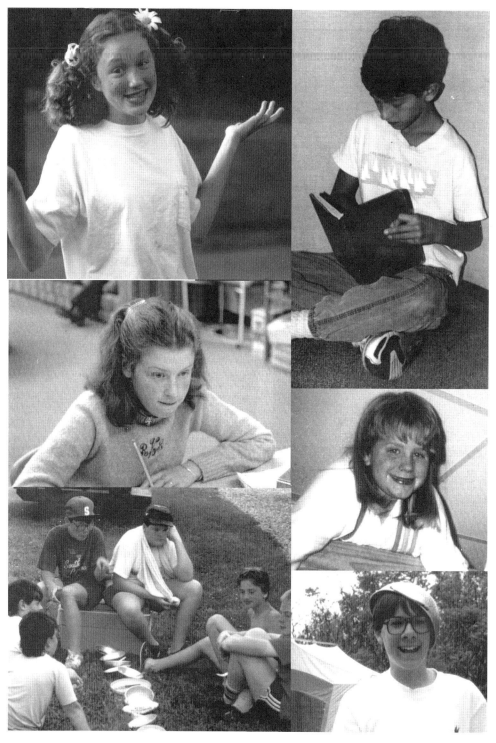

94

VI
Culmination, Reflection, Moving On

Beginning in 1974 after winter break, energy in the Alpha classroom focused on organizing the annual trip. The end-of-the-year adventure provides an opportunity for practical application of skills addressed in the *Essential Behaviors For Learning* document of the Chittenden South Supervisory District. Students identified these skills in their discussion with me as learning how to organize, communicate effectively, make decisions, prioritize, and collaborate with their classmates.

Students take full responsibility organizing the five-day trip. They use the weekly class meeting time to make preparations. Class members sleep in tents, cook meals over outdoor stoves, and study a particular topic. They also talk, laugh, and sing together. In many ways it is a test of the strength of the community that had developed over the year. For it to be successful, everyone has to contribute.

Early in March committees form to begin specific planning. Over the next three months they decide on a site, plan transportation, organize food, write out menus, arrange sleeping conditions, coordinate social events, and choose a theme for study. During late March and April students scurry about town going to supermarkets to compare costs of various food items, while others visit several campgrounds to check out potential sites. The handy ones among them patch holes in tents and assemble equipment packed away after last year's trip. Those assigned to the food preparation committee spend time scouring pots encrusted with spaghetti sauce left from last year when class members rushed through their chores to get to the candlelight ceremony on the final night. As a student told me, even though the groundwork they do for the trip is tiring and difficult, they all feel quite grown up completing their tasks.

Conversations in and out of the classroom are different during this time too. Older students are heard convincing the less brave and adventuresome younger ones that they really do want to go. Parents set aside conversations about grades and progress reports in order to discuss camping gear, Coleman stoves, and sleeping bags. Trips back and forth to school are filled with talk about the flavor of food cooked over an open campfire and the warmth of a down-filled sleeping bag on a cool night. Sentences often begin with "I remember when…" as moms and dads fondly recalled the camping escapades of their youth. Teachers spend countless hours with paperwork, making sure permission forms are filled out, proper authorities notified, and collaborative agreements signed with those agencies contributing equipment and space. When teachers lie awake at night, their thoughts are caught between the worry over possible mishaps and the excitement that comes from seeing the culmination of a year's work. As days grow longer a new momentum is felt in the Alpha classroom. Students work hard to finish their tasks on time, knowing each one's contribution is needed for the trip to succeed. The pressure on students to do their part is subtle but strongly felt. I heard students encouraging other students, even chiding them at times, to complete their work for the trip. Teachers put out gentle reminders, but it is the students themselves who monitor progress.

When departure day arrives in early June, buses line up outside the school. The lawn soon is covered with a colorful array of luggage and sleeping bags. Animated students check their baggage for articles feared forgotten but found in side pockets or hidden between articles of clothing. Parents stand by awkwardly giving last minute advice, wondering how they will manage the week without their sons and daughters. Students have been told by the "packing committee" they are limited to one duffle bag, yet many are waiting with packs slung over their backs or around their waists full of "things to take" that wouldn't fit in the one bag allotment. I heard one student telling a committee member that the bag on her back, which has an interior metal frame and protrudes from the top of her hips to above her head, was not her "suitcase" but rather her "handbag." The bus is quickly loaded with the extra knapsacks stuffed under seats or in any space where students aren't sitting. Some equipment is transported by parents who've agreed to drive to the site—and then leave! This is a student-led, student-enjoyed adventure.

After arriving at the campsite, students move into action—establishing tent sites, staking out boundaries, finding a water supply, figuring out ways to protect food from animal predators—all tasks necessary for living in the wilderness. Older students who have been on trips before show novices how to pitch tents and organize their gear. The kitchen crew arranges cooking utensils in a lean-to designated for this purpose, close to a water source and the availability of space for food preparation. Picnic tables are carted to an open area to create a dining area. Students who are speedy about unpacking their gear are sent in search of wood for nightly bonfires.

By late afternoon on the first day, students are ready for a break from their tasks. Some told me they couldn't believe "how much effort it took" to set up their camp. Stillness enfolds the campground as the Alpha community settles into its home for the next few days. Class members find their own way to rest and relax; some go to their tents for a nap; some are seen with a book sitting by a tree; others pair off and go exploring. "I can't believe we're really here," one friend said to another as they stand on a rise and look back at the settled campground surrounded by a deep blue sky backlit with streaks of orange from the setting sun.

A class meeting led entirely by students is held each morning to discuss activities and assign chores. During this time students and teachers reflect on the successes and failures of the day before. It becomes obvious rather quickly which committees planned well and which need to revise plans if, for instance, tent poles are missing, or if there are "18 pounds of spaghetti and no pot to cook it in." This meeting time is crucial to the successful operation of the trip. Issues are presented and discussed by the entire class. Class members are really quite supportive of each other during these meetings. When problems arise, no one is blamed. They don't get bogged down in conversations about who is at fault. Students work together sorting through difficulties and establishing plans for the day.

This gathering time on the trip is similar to the weekly class meeting held during the year in the Alpha room. The moderator opens the meeting and initiates the discussion. Students bring up problems, talk about them as a group, and offer possible solutions. I found it rather amazing to see how focused and attentive class members were in this place where chipmunks scamper in and out of tents and the wind whirls through the trees. Students listen carefully and look alert. I conclude they have learned well the skills needed to effectively participate in a community and demonstrated them here.

The trips are what Alpha alumni remember most. Years after they've left the classroom they often begin telling me their stories about Alpha with: "My most memorable Alpha experience would have to be the class trip ...," "Most fondly, I love the Alpha trips...," "I guess when I think of Alpha one of the first things that comes to mind is the trip...", or "I could write volumes about the Alpha trips— wow, I'm getting choked up just thinking about it."

The trips are what Alpha alumni remember most.

The weeklong trip did include some "mandatory activities," a term used in several student stories, that were usually dictated by the theme. One alumnus told me about the "business theme" that was the focus of one trip. She said her business consisted of "renting out Coleman stoves, pots, and pans to different restaurants that people were running." Two other students told me how their business was to sponsor a "disco night" and said that they felt "like Donald Trump" after "collecting our money." The class constructed an economy built on a monetary exchange consisting of "Alphians," paper money. Although the disco group felt rich over the success of their entertainment night, they remember how quickly that feeling dissipated "after we paid our bills." During this particular trip students studied buying and selling, profits and margins, learning everything there was to know about monetary exchange.

Each year various traditions are repeated on the trip. A trip song or tape becomes symbolic of the week and reminds students of a specific trip when heard years later. The talent show is a yearly event. Students spoke fondly about these performances; and when I asked them what kinds of talents were part of the show they told me, "basically anything would do—a skit, a song, a lipsych." They did say they took quite a bit of freedom in designing their performances explaining that some of the events were "appreciated more by friends than by teachers." After hearing stories about the talent show from alumni some 30 years out of the program, I was struck by how clearly they could recall details of these performances. Long after the fine points of topics studied during school years were forgotten, specific details about the talent event were remembered. One student began his recollection of this event by creating a picture for me of the place where it happened. "We presented in a pavilion. It had a big opening...there were long windows with no glass on either side of the opening. The windows were about three feet off the ground and had a slanted roof over them." I could picture the place as he continued the description and his story. With classmates and teachers sitting on the ground before them, students performed one-by-one or in small groups, and all received rousing applause as they finished.

Another tradition is the volleyball game that comes near the end of the week and pits teachers against eighth-grade students. While the rest of the class stands by to cheer their classmates, the eighth graders line up on one side of the net with the teachers and adult chaperones on the other. Depending on the number of students in the eighth grade at the time, the teams were sometimes uneven and the game chaotic. An eighth grader described her bewilderment about rules. As she tells the story, the sides were even, seven on each. She thought it was a regular volleyball game and went to pick up the ball that had gone past the boundary line. When she turned around she noticed the teachers were clustered together across the net. They were talking loudly and then turned around saying, "We got it, 1-2-3," and threw water balloons at them. Her teammates quickly caught the ones that did not break and hurled them at the teachers.

Several students talked about the weather conditions. Many of the activities of the trips were connected to the weather during the week, and they varied greatly from year to year. One student told me "we spent some years in 90 degree weather and others when it seemed like 10 degrees. Once in a while in the morning we would have 2-3 inches of snow on the ground or 2-3 inches of water—it all depended on the year." Some years the weather added to the adventure of the trip, and survival became the focus. In June of 1984 torrential rains flooded Vermont fields and rivers. A break in the weather allowed the class to get to Groton State Park and set up a camping site for the anticipated week. By mid-afternoon the rains began again. Students told me it rained so much that they "were flooded out of the area." They found themselves surrounded by water when they woke up on the second morning. Breaking camp in the rain, stuffing wet clothes into duffel bags, eating soggy bread for breakfast, students recall wondering how "they would return home." The planning committee gathered with the teacher to discuss the situation and decided to call for help. Several students told me quite dramatically how the Vermont State Police escorted the buses safely across water-flooded highways, through backcountry roads away from raging rivers, until they reached Shelburne. This adventure reinforced for some students their ability to handle responsibility. One said it "built up her feeling of self-reliance." One class leader used this trip story as an example of how group problem solving works. He ended by saying that "although we didn't know what Mother Nature had in store for us, we all overcame our worries and fears and pulled together to return home safely." He remembers the confidence he gained as his classmates trusted him to get them home.

A decade later, the weather brought an early end to another trip, whose outcome was not as exciting as the previous one but memorable nonetheless. When one alumnus began her story with "There was a heavy downpour…" I thought I had heard this story before and checked with her on the date to be sure it wasn't the trip of '85 she was talking about. She told me it was the '95 trip and proceeded to describe how the class had lasted through a week of rain staying at the campsite. I thought briefly about the cyclical nature of history and longer about how the Alpha curriculum helped students learn to solve problems they confront. It seems a thread that runs through the trip stories links responsibility, collaboration, and confidence with problem solving. Whether the question was one of facing nature's elements or deciding on the study of a theme, students knew how to look at an issue, rely on each other for ideas and support, and come up with a solution. When students told me about the class trips, they often connected parts of those stories to things they had learned during the year saying such things as "as we had done before"…"we knew how to talk together"…"we prioritized just as we had all year." As I listened to them talk I reflected back on the *Essential Behavior Document* outlined as a guide for assessing student growth in Shelburne and thought how many of these behaviors were demonstrated in the stories I was told.

A rite-of-passage in Alpha

The last night of the trip, students sit around a rousing campfire, singing songs and sharing their fondest memories of the past year. It is a time of sharing when "we laugh and cry together." This final time for the entire class to be together is special. Several of them told me, "during this time, we feel closer to each other than we ever were before." Many issues ran through their minds during the last evening depending on their place in the Alpha continuum. The six and seventh graders wonder how they will ever "fill the shoes" of the eighth grade students. Eighth grade students worry about their future and told me they asked themselves repeatedly during the evening if they ever will find "teachers who care so much about our development" or if new classmates will "understand my learning style" and be tolerant of "my ways of exploring problems." Sitting alone by the campfire after the sixth and seventh graders have left, eighth-graders anticipate what they are going to experience in their freshman year of high school. They come together on this night to share parting. One student remembers the anxiety she felt. "As I walked to the lean-to where I would stay for the next two hours, I was confused about what was going to happen next. I was unprepared for the upcoming ceremony."

The Candlelight Ceremony is a ritual for the eighth-grade students on the last night of the trip. It involves "a lot of molten wax" and "even more tears shed." During this time students who are graduating recall who they were when first they entered the Alpha Classroom. One told me "all of us had taken on new identities, ones that nobody knew about before." One by one, passing a lighted candle, students talk about hopes and dreams. The power of this ceremony is readily evident. One student described the connections they all felt with one another and how people who were traditionally slackers came up with Shakespearean quotes, and the stoic male image was shattered as we all sobbed shamelessly. The relationships that had developed over their years in Alpha are apparent as I hear eighth graders discuss the past, laughing at mistakes made and things said, and trying to imagine a future without these friends. They know many will not be together during the next year, but they understand the importance of the bonds they had developed. "I felt so happy and amazed," said one student, "the Alpha class members were all equal and were a real community." As the ceremony winds down, friends wander away, sharing lasting thoughts and experiences. As one former student recalled that evening, she spoke with emotion:

> The two of us had left the traditional Thursday night campfire. We talked about trips we had been on together in the past and the fact that we would never be on another one. The moon had a rainbow aura around it, I remember that clearly. It was the first time I can remember seeing that particular phenomenon. Christina and I were both scared about leaving, about moving on to high school. After a while we joined the teachers at their lean-to and stayed up late talking to them. I think we both felt very grown-up but still very much like scared children.

Moving on while remembering

As the month of June moves toward its end, thoughts in Alpha turn to graduation. Students have returned from the trip, recovered from the end-of-year tests and late-night paper writing, and completed their final projects for the year. Underneath the laughter and confidence expressed by students as they describe their performance on these activities, I hear sounds of uneasiness, and worry as one group prepares to move on and another to advance. I see soon-to-be-graduates talking together in classrooms making plans for summer and fall. They talk about their worries and concerns. Meeting me one day in an empty hallway an eighth grader told me, "I am sad to see school end. I think everyone is sad school is ending even if nobody will admit it. Also I think a lot of others are just as afraid of losing their friends as I am."

On graduation day the front of Shelburne Middle School is a wilderness of bright balloons and colorful flowers made from crumpled paper and attached to the backs of chairs. Students about to graduate, hair combed and dressed in best clothing, sit poised like the adults they are trying to become. One-by-one teachers stand, call a student to the front and tell a favorite story about her or him. The stories make some in the audience laugh and bring tears to the eyes of many. It is a ceremony that represents a community of caring, of teachers and students who know each other well and have been involved in each other's lives. Standing under a tree, listening to the anecdotes, I reflect on stories I have been told that represent the long run of this special educational program called Alpha.

Alpha has gone through many rites of passage since its beginning—sorting its way through tensions and conflicts. At the end of these 33 years it stands solid as a sound educational choice for families in Shelburne. Its composition has solidified with approximately 65 students, grades 6-8, with three teachers and one instructional aide. Alpha continues to involve students in every aspect of the learning process—planning, performing, assessing. Its goal remains to educate students in accord with the same philosophical convictions with which it started:

- To train each child in the skills of responsibility and self-sufficiency.
- To then allow the child to take as much responsibility as can comfortably be handled—no more or less.
- To lead the child to a form of self-discipline that will carry over to those situations where it will be the only discipline worth having.
- To do everything possible to ensure that most of the time the child is happy and free of those outside pressures that really do not need to exist in the belief that she or he will be better able to cope with the pressures that cannot be avoided because of this freedom.
- To encourage the formation of an intellectually curious and creative being, well grounded in basic knowledge and ready to apply it to a field of learning far beyond the usual.

I survey the schoolyard where tall maple trees are in full bloom, and a soft breeze sweeps through the graduation gathering rustling papers held in parents' hands; speaking voices take on the harmonious sounds of the whippoorwill. I see faces of Alpha students, waiting eagerly but confidently for their names to be called, their stories told. I notice them looking through the crowd and catch their smiles as their eyes meet family, friends, teachers. Memories flood across their faces, and mine too, as I remember things they have told me...

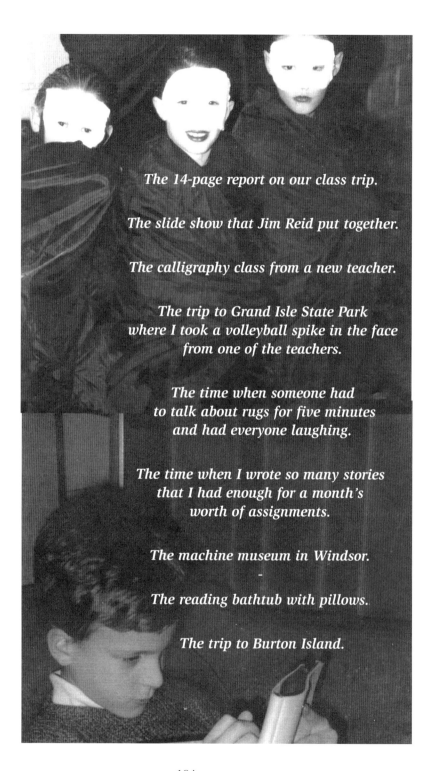

The 14-page report on our class trip.

The slide show that Jim Reid put together.

The calligraphy class from a new teacher.

The trip to Grand Isle State Park
where I took a volleyball spike in the face
from one of the teachers.

The time when someone had
to talk about rugs for five minutes
and had everyone laughing.

The time when I wrote so many stories
that I had enough for a month's
worth of assignments.

The machine museum in Windsor.
-
The reading bathtub with pillows.

The trip to Burton Island.

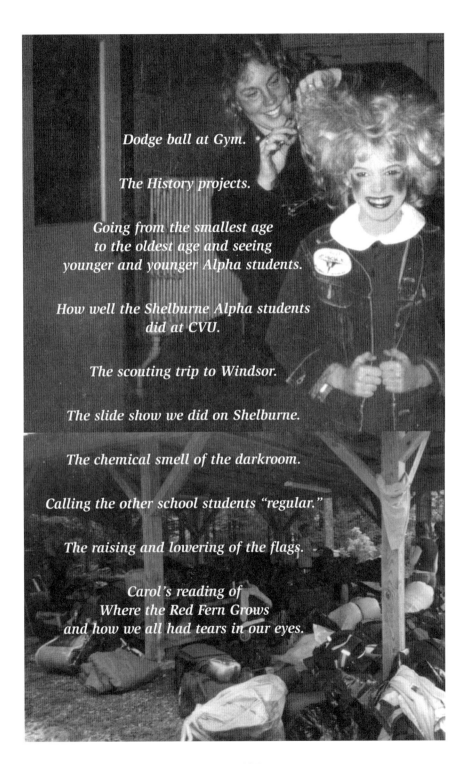

Dodge ball at Gym.

The History projects.

*Going from the smallest age
to the oldest age and seeing
younger and younger Alpha students.*

*How well the Shelburne Alpha students
did at CVU.*

The scouting trip to Windsor.

The slide show we did on Shelburne.

The chemical smell of the darkroom.

Calling the other school students "regular."

The raising and lowering of the flags.

*Carol's reading of
Where the Red Fern Grows
and how we all had tears in our eyes.*

...and Counting

At this writing, more than two years after the study was first completed, Alpha continues to be a 6-8th grade multiaged program in the Shelburne Community School. Currently 65 students and three teachers, Meg O'Donnell, Cynthia Myers, and Joan Cavallo together construct curriculum and activities that address student interest and needs. The centrality of student learning continues to be the hallmark of the program. This team of teachers was a recipient of National Middle School Association's award in 2003 for "Teams That Make a Difference." Two of the teachers have gone on to achieve National Board Certification.

Cynthia Myers, Meg O'Donnell, and Joan Cavallo (L-R) receiving National Middle School Association's award for "Teams That Make a Difference—Increasing Student Achievement" at the 2003 conference in Atlanta.

Pressure from state and regional mandates in the area of standards, measurable learning outcomes, and curricular goals centered around grade levels continue to challenge the Alpha philosophy. In recent years members of the Alpha community have become more intentional about how they address these demands and align them with the mission of the program. Considerable effort has been put into involving administrators, parents, and students in this endeavor. Holding true to the original principles, student voice is at the center of curricular reform and changing structures. In this classroom, students are being heard as they talk about issues, and needs, and what matters to them in the world. For 33 years, Alpha has been guided by the wisdom of students. And it continues to be.

The founder, Jim Reid, in reflecting on Alpha, in a statement made in September 2004 said

> *I am awed by the persistence of Alpha's core, which remains unchanged even as the program itself has matured. John Winton made Alpha's early survival possible, and Carol Smith nurtured it through its adolescence and adulthood. Others of us gave our love and sweat to it, but it is the children who are—and always were—its heart and spirit. They have proved that the desire to help one another springs from a sense of belonging and needs no grade level structure to contain it. The children are Alpha's history, its present, and its future. So raise your glass of camping Kool-Aid and drink a toast. Here's to curious humans, big and small. And here's to teachers everywhere who perform small miracles because they remember what it's all about. ⚹*

EPILOGUE

by Carol Smith

The year 2004 marked Alpha's 33rd year; its commitment to the young adolescents it serves and the belief that the idea of "school" should be about building and nurturing a community of learners is as strong today as it was when what was first called *The Nameless Idea* took flight.

The practices and procedures of this multiage, integrative program have evolved and strengthened over time. The structure of the team has changed with the changing times of the larger school community, and the names of the teachers are different. But the basic principles of democracy, the honoring of student voice, and the active participation of all members of the team—parents, students and teachers as partners in the learning process—remain unchanged from those early days.

In an earlier writing I reflected on the impact of this program with these statements.

> *Alpha has touched the lives of more than 1000 students who are now in high schools, colleges, and out in the world with careers of their own. Some of them are teachers. Some of them work in politics, and government, and health care. Some are artists. Some are craftsmen...and women. Many of them are raising*

families. Despite their differences and distances now, they come from common roots—a shared educational experience in their middle grades years that honored them as learners and supported their growth as individuals. The roots are strong and memories of the journey are rich. Each Alpha student, Alpha parent, and Alpha teacher has added a voice to the shared history that is Alpha.

How lucky I am to have spent my teaching career as a member of the Alpha Team. And how grateful I am to the other Alpha teachers who left "footprints" on its soul and mine, and shared the journey: Jim, Warren, Rich, Dick, Susan, Cyndy, Linda, Kris, Jeanne, Than, Meg, MegO, Nickie, Claire, Cynthia, and Joan. Each of us has been part of something bigger than ourselves, something so important in the lives of Shelburne's children, that this team and all it stands for has survived and thrives today.

Currently education is fraught with controversy. Just when you think things will settle down and teaching and learning can be the true focus of school, another mandate, another demand provides a new challenge. Today, the standards movement and the implications of high stakes testing challenge all teachers nationwide. Decisions about what will and won't be taught in schools and how learning will be measured are being made far from the school room, and much of what actually happens in schools across the nation is scripted by "teaching to the test." Alpha has risen to these challenges; its unwavering commitment to young adolescent learners, together with its belief about how learning happens, has allowed the Alpha program to turn both these dictates into success stories.

The move to student-led portfolio conferences brought strong student voice to the assessment process, and students stepped into the true center of all Alpha practices. While students had been regular participants in their conferences for many years, they now took the lead role as reporters and defenders of their progress and growth. Student-led portfolio conferences became the cornerstone of Alpha's reporting process, and conversations about learning and growth over time became the norm. The shift to student-led portfolio conferences coincided with the state of Vermont's publication of standards for students in grades K-12. Using the district's (Chittenden South) already developed *Essential Behaviors for Learners* as one resource, the state created its *Framework for Standards and Learning Opportunities*. The standards, broken into Fields of Knowledge and Vital Results Standards offered the Alpha Team a structure on which to build and strengthen their portfolios.

The portfolios became collections of work from Alpha's integrated theme studies in the more traditionally defined fields of knowledge: arts and humanities; science, mathematics and technology; and history and social sciences— reorganized to fit with the Vital Results Standards: Communication, Problem Solving, Civic and Social Responsibility, and Personal Development. The portfolio became a way for students to talk about their learning in the context of state standards, and to see how their content work fit into a broader spectrum of learning. Students' weekly goal setting became framed around the Vital Results Standards as well, and assessment and conference conversations used the language of the standards. Alpha students talked intelligently with teachers and each other about the standards with more depth and better understanding than most educators in the state did. It became the language of *their* learning, and they used it every day.

Vermont's *Framework for Standards and Learning Opportunities* supported Alpha in other ways as well. It was organized in multiyear divisions, mirroring nicely Alpha's strong multiage commitment. The standards were broad and conceptual in nature, and supported our work with integrative curriculum themes. Using the questions students had about themselves and the world to focus the studies, we were able to identify and assess performance levels on the state-mandated standards. This became an additional step in the curriculum planning process with students for the year, further focusing their thinking and ours. Standards not addressed through specific themes became the focus of teacher-led seminars, ensuring that Alpha students were well-prepared for their transition to the high school. The state's efforts, in may ways, legitimized the work Alpha was already doing by giving a structure and a language with which to work. The Learning Opportunities, often overlooked in the scramble to meet standards, supported what we saw as best middle level practice, beliefs about the importance of democracy, equity, access for all students, and honoring student voice and choice in the learning process.

It was at this time as well that the entire community school in Shelburne moved to using the New Standards Reference Exam to measure students' abilities in mathematics and reading and language arts. One might think, and many predicted, that without specific content classes, Alpha students would be at a disadvantage in taking this test. Just the opposite proved true. Over the eight years of using these tests, Alpha students outscored their counterparts in Shelburne, the Chittenden South Supervisory Union, and in the state. The success of Alpha students in meeting state standards, along with their high scores on national tests, speaks convincingly about the effects of a progressive, integrated curriculum.

> *The success of Alpha students in meeting state standards, along with their high scores on national tests, speaks convincingly about the effects of a progressive integrated curriculum.*

My 25 years on the Alpha Team have defined and made real in practice all that I believe about education, especially for young adolescents "in the middle." I was lucky enough to be in the right place at the right time when the Alpha Team came to fruition; I thank John Winton for recognizing in me something I had yet to find in myself. Alpha embraces and continues to foster all that is good about public education, when children and learning are the true focus.

Alpha has stayed strong in the face of each challenge—new administrations, new teachers, new standards, new testing, the loss of a student, the loss of its founder, and attacks on its curriculum and stayed true to its beliefs about what's really important for kids:

- Close relationships between teachers and students and their families.
- A viable learning community allowing teachers, students and parents to view learning as a process of growth and deepening understanding that builds over time.
- Students as active participants in all decisions about their learning.
- Opportunities for students to construct personal meaning from their learning.

- A closely aligned team of teaching colleagues (including parents) with whom to share the wonder and excitement of mentoring students as they begin to make sense of this world.

Retiring from the Alpha Team after 25 years was the hardest decision I have ever made. I had it all; teaching was my chosen profession; and I couldn't have had a more exciting, challenging, or rewarding career anywhere else. Now as I work with teachers and schools around the state and the country, I see good people doing good work for kids. **I am encouraged.** I see struggles, and I see survivors. **I am optimistic**. I see teachers and schools unwilling to cave in to the demands and consequences of high stakes testing. I see schools and teachers who know the difference between standards and standardization and I see kids coming out as winners. I am confident about their future. More and more I see teachers looking for ways to make connections to kids and their families, to make connections between kids and the curriculum, and to find connections between school and real life. More and more I see teachers, and parents, and students unwilling to settle for what is now known. They continuously seek a better way. So **I am hopeful**.

Alpha continues, stronger for the work over the years. The Alpha teachers now are inventive and bold, as were those who came before them. They are survivors, creators, inventors, and strong advocates for the young adolescents in their care. And **I am thankful.** 🏃

References

Beane, J. (1990). *A middle school curriculum: From rhetoric to reality* (1st ed.). Columbus, OH: National Middle School Association.

Beane, J. (1997). *Curriculum integration: Designing the core of democratic education.* New York: Teachers College Press.

Brown, K., & Martin, A. (1989). Student achievement in multi-grade and single grade classes. *Education Canada, 29* (2), 11-13.

Carnegie Council on Adolescent Development. (1989). *Turning points: Preparing American youth for the 21st century.* New York: Carnegie Corporation.

Gutierrez, R., & Slavin, R. (1992). Achievement effects of non-graded elementary schools: A best evidence synthesis. *Review of Educational Research, 62* (4), 333-334.

Miller, B. (1990). A review of quantitative research on multi-grade instruction. *Journal of Research in Rural Education, 7* (1), 1-8.

Pavan, B. (1992). The benefits of non-graded schools. *Educational Leadership, 50* (2), 22-25.

Pipher, M. (1994). *Reviving Ophelia: Saving the selves of adolescent girls.* New York: Putnam.

Related Resources
on Middle Level Curriculum,
Assessment, and Organization

Alexander, W. (1995). *Student-oriented curriculum: Asking the right questions.* Columbus, OH: National Middle School Association.

Atwell, N. (1998). *In the middle: New understandings about writing, reading, and learning.* Portsmouth, NH: Boynton/Cook.

Arnold, J., & Stevenson, C. (1998). *Teacher's teaming handbook: A middle level planning guide.* Orlando, FL: Harcourt Brace and Co.

Austin, T. (1994). *Changing the view: Student led conferences.* Portsmouth, NH: Heinemann.

Beane, J. (1993). *A middle school curriculum: From rhetoric to reality* (2nd ed.). Columbus, OH: National Middle School Association.

Bergstrom, K, Bishop, P., & Carr, J. (2001). *Living and learning in the middle grades: The dance continues.* Westerville, OH: National Middle School Association.

Boomer, G. (1992). *Negotiating the curriculum.* New York: Falmer Press.

Braunger J., & Hart-Landsberg, S. (1994). *Crossing Boundaries: Exploring integrative curriculum.* Portland, OR: Northwest Regional Educational Laboratory.

Brazee, E., & Capelluti, J. (1995). *Dissolving boundaries, Toward an integrative curriculum.* Columbus, OH: National Middle School Association.

Caine, R., & Caine, G. (1991). *Making connections: Teaching and the human brain.* Alexandria, VA: Association for Supervision and Curriculum Development.

Daniels, H. (1994). *Literature circles: Voice and choice in the student-centered classroom.* Portland, ME: Stenhouse Publishers.

George, P., & Lounsbury, J. (2000). *Making big schools feel small: Multiage grouping, looping, and schools-within-a-school.* Westerville, OH: National Middle School Association.

Gibbons, M. (1990). *The walkabout papers.* Vancouver, BC: EduServe, Inc.

Jackson, A., & Davis, G. (2000). *Turning points 2000: Educating adolescents for the 21st century.* New York: Teachers College Press.

Kenney, M., O'Donnell, M., & Smith. C. (1995). Student-led parent conferences. *VAMLEFocus.* Johnson, VT: Vermont Association for Middle Level Education.

Kohn, A. (2000). *The case against standardized testing: Raising the scores, ruining the schools.* Portsmouth, NH: Heinemann.

Kohn, A. (1993). *Punished by rewards.* Boston: Houghton Mifflin.

Knowles, T., & Brown, D. (2000). *What every middle school teacher should know.* Portsmouth, NH: Heinemann.

Lipsitz, J. (1984). *Successful schools for young adolescents.* New Brunswick, NJ: Transaction Books.

Lounsbury, J., & Vars, G. (1978). *A curriculum for the middle school years.* New York: Harper & Rowe.

Lounsbury, J. (1992). *Connecting the curriculum through interdisciplinary instruction.* Columbus, OH: National Middle School Association.

National Educational Association, Teacher to Teacher Series. (1996) Integrated Thematic Teaching.

National Middle School Association. (2003). *This we believe: Successful schools for young adolescents.* Westerville, OH: National Middle School Association.

Perrone, V. (Ed.) (1991). *Expanding student assessment.* Alexandria, VA: Association for Supervision and Curriculum Development.

Springer, M. (1998). *Watershed: A successful voyage into integrated learning.*Columbus, OH: National Middle School Association.

Stevenson, C. (1998). *Teaching 10 to 14 year olds* (2nd ed.). New York: Longman Publishing.

Stevenson, C., & Carr, J. (1992). *Integrated studies in the middle grades: Dancing through walls.* New York: Teachers College Press.

Vars, G. (1997). Student concerns and standards, too. *Middle School Journal, 28* (4), 54-57.

Vermont Framework for Standards and Learning Opportunities. (Revised, 1996). Montepelier, VT: State Department of Education.

Wiggins, G. (1998). *Understanding by design.* Alexandria, VA: Association for Supervision and Curriculum Development.

Zemelman, S., Daniels, H., & Hyde, A. (1998). *Best practice learning: New standards for teaching and learning in America's schools.* Portsmouth, NH: Heinemann.